LABOR: America's Two-Faced Movement

LABOR:
America's
Two-Faced
Movement

HERRICK S. ROTH

FIRST EDITION

 PETROCELLI/CHARTER   NEW YORK 1975

Library of Congress Cataloging in Publication Data

Roth, Herrick S   1916-
    Labor.

    Includes index.
    1. Trade-unions--United States. I. Title.
HD6508.R6517   331.88'0973   75-15682
ISBN 0-88405-311-3
ISBN 0-88405-312-1 pbk.

Dedication

*To George Vardaman, who convinced me that my understanding of
trade union structure had not been stated in the terms that he
had on several occasions heard me state it; to my wife, Marjorie,
whose patience and insistence finally made me set aside the time
to do it, and to Zelda Bransted, Sue Cunningham, and Sally Sherwood,
who gave their professional time without compensation to make
certain that the manuscript was transferred to typewritten
translation, assembled, and indexed—because they all shared the
same beliefs about this text as did the man who needled me to do it.*

Contents

Preface

My involvement with the American labor movement has been direct and daily since World War II. My experience has also been varied: organizing unions for the first time; bargaining contracts, proposing the right of public workers to bargain collectively; supporting or disputing with top labor leadership from all corners of the nation; serving in a legislative body where labor stands in constant judgment; pursuing trade union interests in the same legislative lobbies; mediating and arbitrating; walking the picket lines, leading boycott activities for the disadvantaged—my union life has been rich and rewarding.

Writing reports and articles, and in discussions over the years, I have been able to stand aside and view what the trade union movement is all about. Now, in this book, I have a chance to present in an extended, coherent analysis, the past events, present characteristics, and future prospects of American trade unions.

This book does not represent a consensus. It is a review of my own judgments about an institution that will survive as long as America survives. In fact, unions may have more to do with America's ability to survive than any single other private body in our land.

The great majority of adult Americans—including union members and their leaders—do not fully understand what American trade unions really are or yet could be. Let me explain. Labor is composed of two structural fundamentals: separate unions and a movement. Even though the membership of all the unions in the nation make up the movement, it is easier for the member to identify with his union than with the movement. On the other hand, the nonmember may find it easier to identify the movement but not to distinguish the differences among the many unions.

This book concerns itself with both the unions and the movement

—how labor is organized, or not organized, in America. It is my perspective, not a review of studies or historical statements of others.

Since I have lived much of what I set forth here, I admit to some prejudgments, yet I have not ignored the demands of objectivity. I consider the descriptions and conclusions of this book to be generally valid enough to cause the reader to review, weigh, and evaluate his own judgments about American labor.

I state this review of contemporary American Labor as a trade unionist with an in-house point of view. I believe that a trade union is in a position to improve job conditions for the worker. Labor also has much to contribute to the quality of American life. I believe that a union shop is just as basic to American welfare as full-citizen commitment to the nation.

Who are trade unionists? To answer that question, consider the following: Earned income is that derived by people who work for someone else to make a living. Unearned income comes from return on investments, if any. To protect unearned income, investors do not form unions. To protect the right to earn income at a decent rate under safe conditions, jobholders often form or join unions. If they do, they are known as trade unionists.

By forming into groups, workers gain some degree of influence over their own destinies and, yes, over the destinies of others. How labor exercises power and what kind of power it has are related to American progress. Labor must be careful to utilize power based on democratic involvement and decision making by the rank and file. Autocracy in an institution eventually leads to the crumbling of the institution. Its power becomes powerless. By contrast, an institution whose leaders show humility and compassion is probably one that utilizes the processes and thus the power of democracy to the fullest.

American labor has had the choice between these kinds of institutional structure and leadership on many occasions; it has usually opted for open democracy. I suspect that it will continue to do so and better serve people by their own involvement at the critical junctures ahead.

In this book, I relate why I believe this. In the process, I deal with the structures, the leadership, and the respective strengths and shortcomings of trade union America. The aspirations and hopes of workers rest with these very same trade unions.

1

Labor's Two Faces

The title of this chapter sounds derogatory. It is not. Labor is not simple to explain. But labor has two basic faces. That can be explained. What results from having two faces can be explained. That's what this book is all about. The title is properly descriptive.

Neither of labor's faces is intended to deceive the other. This is not a matter of talking out of both sides of the mouth. Each face relates to a different function of the body of trade union America.

One face relates to the function of the "movement," where labor hangs it all together. The face appropriately reflects that the movement doesn't hang together all that well. "Solidarity Forever" is the song and symbol of the movement. Occasionally, it can be sung with feeling and meaning. Its infrequent rendition indicates that things aren't just that solid.

The other face portrays the bargaining function of labor. This is the economic well-being of the individual worker, his bread and butter. This second face portrays the process of collective bargaining. The substance dealt out through that process runs between the poles; the process and the structure surrounding that process, however, usually have a common face. This is the basic face of American labor.

If American trade unionism can be faulted seriously, the fault is that the face of movement is paled by the face of bargainer, and the two faces often weaken rather than complement each other.

Labor: No Monolith

Labor is a mixed bag. Its two faces tell us so. Yet, this assertion does not square with popular opinion.

Why do I say that labor is a mixed bag? There are times and

places where it would appear that unions are strong. Some people would say that they wield too much power on such occasions. Then they reach the next conclusion. Labor speaks with one voice. Labor is a monolith.

No such thing.

Labor in America is a multitude of unions, big unions and small unions; big unions with many local unions; other big unions with fewer and fewer local unions that are getting bigger and bigger by merger; small unions with a multiplicity of even smaller local unions; small unions with only a few local unions.

The watchword for all of these unions is *autonomy*. Occasionally, some of these unions stretch the point. Autonomy is only at the top of those unions. But generally it is true—there is autonomy. For instance, the Retail Clerks international union is autonomous and quite separate from the Meat Cutters international union. This is true even though many of their members work side by side in the local supermarket. They don't necessarily make their union decisions together. They are autonomous, one from the other.

Autonomy at the Local Level

Retail Clerks Local 1 may act completely differently from Retail Clerks Local 2. They are in different areas, first of all, and don't necessarily compare notes. Even if they do, they don't have to. They are autonomous of each other even though both belong to the same national (usually called "international" because the Retail Clerks International Association (RCIA) can charter local unions in both the United States and Canada).

The international union offers something in common to each of the locals—they both are chartered—they both are affiliated—they both belong. But down at the local union level, each is autonomous from the other within the structure of the international union.

Local decisions—election of local officers, the number of and training of business agents, the kind of headquarters each local has, the internal communications—all are the pride, joy, and stylish structure of each local union.

If the local's officers aren't found to be corrupt, if the local is not being mismanaged, or if the local's officers are not failing to enforce a collectively bargained agreement, then the international union will find it difficult to interfere with how the local union does business. That local is more autonomous than even its international union constitution says it is.

Even if the illustration here does not square precisely with what might happen in the union known as RCIA, it is relatively accurate when applied across approximately 125 international and national unions in the United States. Collectively, they have 49,000 local unions.

Sometimes—in fact, usually—a local union has a bargained agreement with more than one employer. Sometimes, the local union and the same employer have more than one contract with each other —a basic, or master, agreement and a specialized, or supplementary, agreement. Sometimes, it has no agreement at all with an employer (usually in the public sector—that is, government).

LABOR, THE BARGAINING FACE

The 49,000 local unions have over a quarter of a million different agreements covering almost 18,000,000 full-time American workers in nonfarm employment. Most of these agreements bespeak autonomy. The local unions have usually bargained the contract. They have bargained autonomously, with or without the help and expertise of the parent union. These contracts cover well over half of the organized work force of America.

Autonomy proclaims "To each his own."

This is the face of labor, the bargainer.

Even if we said that every single one of the 125 international unions established one inflexible way for its locals to do business, there could still be 125 different modes of operation. The vertical structure of trade unions in America provides for almost absolute separation of these unions from each other. Solidarity is not overriding, is not of first priority. Solidarity, if at all, comes from top to bottom of each union. Solidarity is not horizontal—is not "side by side," seeking the same cherished goal. Only sometimes is it so, when each national and international union comes face to face with the same problem and recognizes it.

Transportation—An Example of Mixed Bag

Take transportation as an example of a basic industry in America.

On the waterfront, there is not one maritime union. Among the longshoremen there are AFL-CIO affiliates, the International Longshoremen's Association (ILA), in the East, Gulf, and St. Lawrence ports, among others, and the International Longshoremen's and Warehousemen's Union (ILWU) in the Pacific ports.

And there are more: National Maritime Union of America; International Organization of Masters, Mates and Pilots; Marine & Shipbuilding Workers; National Marine Engineers' Beneficial Association; Seafarers International Union and two of its independent offshoots, the Inlandboatmen of the Pacific and the Atlantic Gulf Lakes and Inland Waters District.

This list may not be complete, but it is indicative of the autonomies that exist. There is not always a clear line of jurisdiction among the unions.

The railroad mergers in recent years have not been just of rail lines, but of unions, too. There are still separate unions: railroad signalmen; railroad yardmasters; railway clerks (they also deal in water carrier, bus, air, and trucking jurisdictions); railway carmen; train dispatchers; and the union that merged the railroad engineers, conductors, brakemen, enginemen, firemen, oilers—United Transportation Union (UTU).

There are unions that deal primarily with buses and trucks (both over-the-road and local delivery). One name stands out here, Teamsters (International Brotherhood of Teamsters, Chauffeurs, Warehousemen and Helpers of America). The urban area transit systems are serviced in different areas primarily by two unions: Amalgamated Transit Union and Transport Workers Union of America. ATU also has the long-haul buses in many parts of the nation; TWU even deals with some airline personnel.

In the airways, in addition to those already mentioned, there is International Air Line Pilots Association (ALPA), holding the elite spot on the list. There are also the Aircraft Mechanics Fraternal Association, the International Air Line Employees Association, and the Air Line Dispatchers.

In this area, though, unions that once started out on a different course have managed major jurisdictional representation along the commercial air routes. The Teamsters represent all classifications of employees with one major airline. The International Association of Machinists and Aerospace Workers (IAM) represents more than half the major U.S. airlines in all types of aircraft servicing—not just the mechanical and body maintenance of the multimillion-dollar airships. Once upon a time the Railway Clerks worked only on railroads. Now, their often expanded jurisdiction is described by their title of the moment: Brotherhood of Railway, Airline and Steamship Clerks, Freight Handlers, Express and Station Employees, AFL-CIO.

So much for the example, transportation and unions in America. These unions have as their reason for existence a common trait— the face of labor, the bargainer.

Autonomy prevails. A detailed description of the leadership structure, multicrossed lines of jurisdictions, size, and the frequently dissimilar kinds of membership would prove only that the workers who belong to these employee organizations live in the mixed bag of trade unions, American style. This is one face of labor, a unique and rather tight structure fashioned to keep the vertical autonomies separate and apart. Each union is its own. That is its prime face.

LABOR'S OTHER FACE

To the outsider, this is the face that seems most apparent. It's the face of the movement. It's the face of the "House of Labor." To the insider, however, this is the lesser face—the face in the shadow.

The A.F. of L. and the C.I.O.

The AFL-CIO presents the general face of labor, in spite of the fact that it does not include the two largest unions in the nation, the Teamsters and the Auto Workers.

The teamsters were often in the spotlight when that union was very much a part of the labor movement. They were a cornerstone of many jurisdictions in the old American Federation of Labor. They were still the number-one union in size when the A.F. of L. and the Congress of Industrial Organizations merged in December, 1955. The new, hyphenated name, AFL-CIO, was significant then and remains so. The old A.F. of L. and the newer CIO moved closer together but not quite all the way.

From the former CIO, the International Union of United Automobile, Aerospace and Agricultural Implement Workers of North America (UAW) was the largest—just short of the Teamsters. Its leader, who succeeded to the late Phil Murray's guiding hand at the helm of the CIO, was Walter Reuther.

Reuther is generally acknowledged as the man who had to put the greater gift on the table of sacrifice during the several years prior to 1955 to achieve merger. The larger house in the divided movement had to give less, but even the A.F. of L. under George Meany's new presidency had to give some. Just to have Meany talk face to face with a CIO leader was a decided change from both the attitude and practice of his predecessor, William Green.

The New Hope of the New Face

The early 1950s produced a new era of hope for labor's other face. The A.F. of L. and the CIO became the AFL-CIO.

Ostensibly there were many reasons for merger. In fact, there was really one overriding drive that pushed merger to reality. There was an unquestionable need to speak with a united political voice in the top echelons of government—the White House and the Congress.

In 1935, President Roosevelt signed a key New Deal measure, the National Labor Relations Act (NLRA), often called the Wagner Act in honor of its chief proponent in the Senate. Less than a decade and a half later, a conservative Congress passed the Taft-Hartley amendments to the act. This drove all unions to a common ground. They hoped to shore up a common face. Organized labor wanted to undo part of the Taft-Hartley. Their separate efforts were not achieving the undoing. Thus, the nation's two largest union organizations joined forces to achieve their purpose.

In a relative sense, the Teamsters had never distinguished themselves in the political arena. They hearkened to but did not seem attuned to the old adage of Sam Gompers, founder of the A.F. of L. Gompers talked about bargaining, all right. But Gompers perceived that there were friends and there were enemies of trade unions (and of workers) in government at all levels. He also understood that until public officials were friendly to organized labor in America, unions weren't going to do much bargaining or engage in effective strikes by manning peaceful picket lines. He admonished all working people, but especially trade unionists, to "elect our friends and defeat our enemies."

The Largest Unions: Different Political Styles

The Teamsters, the largest union, was not out front in the political trenches on general election days; the second largest, the UAW, was. It had made the CIO the target of both hate and fear campaigns through its Political Action Committee (PAC).

In 1955, Walter Reuther was at his most eloquent in dreaming out loud about what 16,000,000 American trade unionists in a work force of about 65,000,000 could do together in "electing our friends and defeating our enemies."

The Teamsters were soon to be forced to leave the common face behind. George Meany realized that when his old friend Dan Tobin left the Teamsters' top chair to Dave Beck and then Jimmy Hoffa. Meany let it be known that the Teamsters were adding to the public tarnish that made the total movement the "fall guy" of the antilabor forces in America.

Ethics: The Measuring Stick

The AFL-CIO at the start of merger set up an ethical practices code. It was one of the few places where the over 140 national and international unions agreed to accept a common stance and be judged by each other. Although not made binding by the AFL-CIO constitution (at least not directly so), it was heartening within the movement to find one place where all the autonomous bodies agreed to be bound by a moral commitment.

Meany, the first and only president of the merged organization, stood the measuring stick of the agreed-upon code beside the Teamsters (and the Bakery and Confectionery Workers) in the interval between the founding and the second constitutional AFL-CIO Convention (1957). With Reuther standing by his side on that one, the Teamsters were excommunicated from the AFL-CIO. Expelled! The 1957 debate was heated and generally healthy.

Through his convention committee, Meany zeroed in on Jimmy Hoffa. If the Teamsters thought they could muster one-third of the vote—all they needed to avoid revocation of AFL-CIO affiliate status —they were wrong. They started with their own favorable handicap, 10 percent of the roll call vote. About 140 other unions had 90 percent. Moving the needed one-fourth of that 90 percent in support of the Teamsters didn't seem insurmountable, especially when the debate focused on whether or not the accusation against one or two top leaders was cause to disaffiliate over a million and one-half members down the line. Just the loss of 10 percent of the AFL-CIO's revenue potential in the new federation would have jolted lesser leaders than Meany and Reuther.

But the Teamsters were cut adrift, by the required vote, only two years after the movement had put itself together. In terms of membership in their own international union, apparently they have not suffered. In the past 16 years, they have increased their independent status by a reportedly net gain of 20 percent in membership.

In spite of Meany's dogged determination to enforce an AFL-CIO policy and constitutional provision, the Teamsters continue to be local affiliates of AFL-CIO building trades councils in many areas. In one sense, the doggedness is more pronouncement than fact. No jurisdiction affiliated with the AFL-CIO seems to suffer any disciplinary action for illegally permitting and/or inviting Teamsters' direct affiliation at the state and local levels.

Thus, the Teamsters are both inside and outside the AFL-CIO. Officially out at the top, they are officially and unofficially in the local arenas of labor activity—especially the building trades and food councils. The building trades depend upon the strong support of the construction truck drivers and the construction materials delivery drivers. The food councils (retail clerks, meatcutters, bakery workers, machinists, stationary engineers, etc.) deal with Teamsters on the delivery docks and in the supermarket warehouses.

However, at the movement level—at the political level—the Teamsters are independent, often at odds with the AFL-CIO and sometimes not around at all. Officially, they aren't there as part of the other face.

UAW—the successor to the title of the AFL-CIO's largest union in 1957—managed to stay on board the merger wagon another ten years. Let's review that period.

The AFL-CIO set up an executive council of vice-presidents to meet periodically and review the administration and activities of the federation. Also on the council were two full-time executive officers, a president and a secretary-treasurer. George Meany, as the leader of the larger A.F. of L., assumed the chair as president from the start. There have been two secretary-treasurers since—reputedly Meany's choices. No one, including Walter Reuther, considered the secretary-treasurer's position as number two in the federation. Reuther was simply proclaimed as the number two officer, even though only a vice president. There was and is no such office as first vice-president. But Reuther was continually recognized by the media, in the AFL-CIO, and at the biennial conventions as number two.

It is beyond the scope of this book to discuss whether or not Reuther really believed that his own more aggressive, broadly based trade union and public policy positions would make him Meany's successor. Meany seemed to portray Reuther's role increasingly as that of an adversary. Many who were close to Reuther from the days of the sit-down strikes in the 1930s to his untimely death in an air crash in the late 1960s offer contradictory opinions on his status and influence at the top of the AFL-CIO. They all knew and thought that he ought to have succeeded Meany within the decade that followed merger.

Reuther's Final AFL-CIO Moves

At the 1965 AFL-CIO convention in San Francisco, Reuther made his final appearance at the podium. Although he had some things to say about the domestic economy and problems during the course of that convention, his most articulate and detailed analysis was saved for foreign policy. The issue was Vietnam.

George Meany knew it was a war against communists. Walter Reuther was not of the same mind. They reached a compromise; Reuther almost sorrowfully belabored the position that the AFL-CIO had to support the Johnson administration's military role in Southeast Asia. Reuther's UAW colleague and secretary-treasurer, Emil Mazey, had to deliver Reuther's and the UAW's real position, that the war in Vietnam was not in America's best interests. The position was the opposite of Meany's. But the compromise won out substantially; Mazey and the UAW and Reuther were literally moved aside; and even some of the former CIO international union delegations supported the compromise.

That compromise had embedded in it the emphasis on standing firm against communism and achieving peace with honor—a position that was closer to the Richard Nixon whom the AFL-CIO leaders never thought could be President of the United States than it was to LBJ's. The lace that made the compromise support possible by Reuther was embroidered as the fringe—namely, the need to bring the war to an early end and the confidence of American trade unions that LBJ could accomplish that purpose.

Reuther left the 1965 convention as a defeated leader—one who might otherwise have challenged Meany's leadership on two bases: first, that the AFL-CIO had not given much of itself to organize the unorganized work force over a ten-year period; second, that the worldwide foreign policy program of the AFL-CIO was too anticommunist to be realistic, including the alleged connections of the CIA to AFL-CIO-backed organizational programs in Latin America.

If Reuther had challenged Meany in a direct election bid for the AFL-CIO presidency, it might have enlivened the good health of the labor movement. Reuther would have lost that 1965 bid, but it might have made him a realistic challenger at the 1967 convention.

Master Plan Without Spokesmen

When 1967 came, the UAW sent a master plan resolution on the new priorities for both America and the AFL-CIO to the convention in Bal Harbour, Florida. That's all they sent—the resolution. It is true that Reuther and his top colleagues were engaged in one of the toughest rounds of bargaining that they had ever faced with the big three automakers. But to say that no one from the largest union in the AFL-CIO could come to represent the 1,400,000 in its ranks was hardly a reasonable stance.

Actually, the UAW was in the process of withdrawing from its affiliation with the AFL-CIO. Whether or not George Meany knew this, it was easy for him to chant his caustic wit to the delegates. When questioned about whether or not the UAW resolution was to be placed on the floor, one of Meany's responses indicated that if "Walter" was really serious about that resolution, his presence was the way to show it.

Reuther's presence was not registered in 1967. His absence haunted some, was derided by others, was mourned by a few, and was noted for what it really meant—he was out. UAW was out because Meany knew that the other industrial unions were not going to follow Reuther out. UAW was out because the dreams of a Walter Reuther could not square with what was the reality of the AFL-CIO.

The exodus was mutually acceptable, even though it gave George Meany a chance to exercise his own pungent eloquence in a forum that he feels best suited to his style. He seemingly enjoyed pointing out as often as possible that it was Reuther who had shirked his commitments to the AFL-CIO—not the AFL-CIO failing to back up the Reuther dream.

For quite different reasons and with an entirely different set of facts and game plans, Meany zeroed in on Reuther as pointedly as he had on Hoffa. The UAW per capita did not come in. As a union, it became technically suspended for arrearages in monthly payments. In 1968, Meany's executive council declared the UAW officially removed.

But the Movement Lives

The other face of labor, the movement, is very firmly alive. It still controls no union's bargaining table. It still is almost a sole voice before the committees and within the lobbies of Congress.

During Richard Nixon's presidency, it was not the sole voice of labor in the White House. When labor as a movement was asked to be on pay and price boards, the AFL-CIO was in no position to suggest who all the members should be—even with 115 unions with over 13,000,000 members among them. The movement—the other face—had to let the two biggest unions join the face, and the UAW and the Teamsters were there—disproportionately there.

This discussion would be incomplete without mention of the two principal independent unions that have not been part of the movement's face for several decades. One is the Pacific area ILWU (Harry Bridges' longshoremen); the other is the United Mine Workers of America (UMWA). The latter union gave birth to most of the early leaders of the great American industrial unions, and the second president of the A.F. of L., William Green, came from its ranks.

While Green was heading up the A.F. of L., which was dominated by craft unions, his union brother who had moved from the coal mines to the steel mills to organize the key basic industrial union in America, the United Steelworkers, headed up the old CIO. He was Philip Murray. He and Bill Green didn't merge anything in their time, but their basic union, the United Mine Workers of America, belonged to one or the other of the divided houses over the years.

The Key Independent: UMWA

Although the UMWA was led through its early years of trial and bloodshed by a man whose honor matched his fortitude, John Mitchell, it is more closely linked to the name of John L. Lewis. When it came to the movement, John L. acted precipitously. From the last time that he scribbled "We disaffiliate" in the 1930s to the great rebirth of democracy in the UMWA in the 1970s, the UMWA has not been the largest but might be described as the most significant of the independents. Even though it probably has more members who are believers in the movement—in the other face—than any union in America today, it has only one official face—its own. That face directly confronts one of the great poverty areas of the nation, the coalfields.

So labor has two faces—the hard bargainer, the one that delivers on bread-and-butter issues, is out front. Here it is the individual union that comes first. The other face is the portrayal of labor's community profile—its public eyes and voice. But if that other face is just a bit pale, it's because four of America's key unions, measured by variable standards relating to size and vigor, don't bring their life blood to its support.

Labor solidarity? Labor, the monolith? Hardly so, with its many faces. But the two faces that stand out are labor as the bargainer and labor as the movement. And if these two faces have anything in common, it is that they belong to the same members.

The Member Wears Two Faces

We call the member a trade unionist. Beyond that, it's difficult to generalize about that person. If we could, it would be easier to talk about solidarity. Then, if he were worried about monolithic power, the reader would be squirming.

As this trade unionist wears his two faces, he finds on occasion that the face of the movement sets the pace for the face of the bargainer. If the bargainer gets in trouble, he hopes the movement can bail him out—on the picket line or in the halls of government. If the movement is ready for the bargainer's plea, it helps; if it is not, the hope for solidarity is temporarily or permanently shattered. When the movement is weak, regardless of the strength of any bargainer, its ability to aid is also weak—and like being bad, that makes his movement face horrid.

Thus, in the early 1970s, the movement found itself in some horrid times—in Congress, in the White House, on the picket lines, in the political arena. It hadn't even the courage or the strength of judgment to help the rank-and-file movement in the independent UMWA to overthrow corruption at many levels of its union.

If UMWA under Tony Boyle had been in the AFL-CIO, the face of labor's movement in the early 1970s might not have been shining so brightly in attacking the Teamsters under Hoffa. Additionally, Hoffa had not then been sentenced by a federal court. If UMWA had been on board, the Yablonski murders might have forced the AFL-CIO to act as a movement to clear up the unsavory lack of democracy in UMWA. Instead, that union's members had to get protection from the federal courts.

Movement May Get Face-Lifting from Bargaining

It could be that in the balance of the 1970s, the movement's face will need to get a lift from the prime face of labor, the bargainer; from the UMWA and its new and almost unbridled spirit and action of democracy; from the Steelworkers and the new efforts at continuous bargaining to avoid strikes in the most basic of industries; and from the likes of the Oil, Chemical and Atomic Workers (OCAW), which seeks to cover environmental issues by bargained contract. OCAW knows the dangerous workplaces and communities where oil- and chemical- and radiation-production facilities are often spewing out life-shortening elements.

If, while one face seems to fail, the other might bring necessary strength, we have to recall that both faces belong to the same persons—the trade unionists. What is this trade unionist all about? How can we best define him or her?

What a Trade Unionist Is

A trade unionist believes in the right of anyone who works for a living to organize and bargain collectively for his job rights—and, obviously, for the job rights of all who work with him for a common employer. (Throughout the book we follow general practice and refer to workers by the masculine pronoun, avoiding she/he and his/her. The reader should of course be reminded that there are approximately four million American women in trade unions.) The unionist is not just a believer; he joins with his fellow workers in a union; he pays his dues; he is willing to go on strike against his employer; he is not about to let his union go down the drain if he can help it. With it all, he is not necessarily anti-employer, even though he may say so on more than one occasion.

Just about everything else revolves around this rather simple description of a trade unionist. If he tries to start his own union, he finds out what it is all about, and this tends to strengthen his trade union determination. Who his leaders are depend upon how many of his colleagues share this sense of determination.

If he has been handed his union and his working conditions on a platter, it takes a lot longer for him to decide that he can even call himself a trade unionist. And if neither his employer nor his union leadership even introduces him to his management-labor agreement when he first comes to his job, he may be as indifferent to his union as he is to whether or not his employer makes a profit.

Since the trade unionist is simply a human being in the job market, his degree of understanding and interest and commitment varies from abject apathy to passionate belief.

Determining the Trade Unionist's Face

Since he is just a human, the character of a worker's trade union face often depends on factors that he looks upon as beyond his control. Even when he has on his bargaining face, he notes that his union adapts that face to the kind of business that it faces at the bargaining table. His bargaining face is often distinctively different—in contour and texture—as he faces different managements: one for government, another for steel, a third for rubber, yet another for publishing houses, jaw set number five for construction, and so on.

To put it another way, the business of producing steel is not that of automaking or of printing or of homebuilding. Each face is differently lined.

As noted earlier, there are at least a quarter-million written agreements bearing joint signatures signifying that management and labor have faced each other and been able to conclude what their faces found in common. Some estimates, adding verbal agreements and letters of understanding or intent, add to that number another 250,000.

We might say that the average bargaining agreement in America covers about 300 to 400 persons. Thus, there are some average faces and there are some variations in those average faces of the trade unionist as bargainer.

Don't Bet on the Average

Averages are misleading, so don't buy them.

For one thing, employers are getting bigger. Some employers want basic agreements across a total work force—particularly in production industries like basic steel. Unions sometimes seek the broad-based basic contract, too.

Regardless of who seeks it or who seeks to resist it, an industry like steel has a basic agreement covering the big ten companies. Production and maintenance employees under the "basic" probably total around 400,000 on any one day. As the bargainers on both sides of the table become more sophisticated, they do their best to make bargaining a continuous experience so that neither strikes nor lockouts need to be figured into the economics of how basic steel plans its production and inventory schedules.

This kind of bargaining goes on at top levels with large and highly involved wage-policy committees, representatively chosen by local unions that are located in every home community where basic steel's plants are situated—and that's in every major river valley and shoreline of America.

The final decisions on the basic agreement are made at the conference tables in New York and Pittsburgh. But if the wage-policy committees have done their best in understanding both the top leadership of their own union and what management does in the respective plants, then the secret-ballot ratification from the members is for real. In the end, then, no one really drives a bad bargain.

Bargaining patterns like steel's are not necessarily paralleled by other big producing industries. The big three automakers (GM, Ford, Chrysler) do not bargain together. Whether or not the Auto Workers or the rivalry among the three top producers has created this situation is debatable.

The point is that the union bargains industry-wide, but with one corporation at a time. The fourth producer, American Motors, is treated to the "fruits of the bargaining table" already produced by one or more of the other three when their contracts are completed.

Business Patterns Shape Bargaining Procedures

These two large industries, steel and auto, producing and creating both products and wealth in America, have caused bargaining to fit the patterns of the respective industries. Thus, unions have adapted themselves to the manner by which each of their respective employers does business. The basic bargaining process is geared to that pattern; any supplementary agreements for the local community plant or zone get more input from the individual members. This factor, too, is very important, because the contract will not work unless the members are pleased.

There are other contrasts in styles and methods of bargaining everywhere in business where unions are certified to bargain.

American business makes labor a mixed bag. Workers, themselves, mix up their bags. Trade union structure either creates or maintains the mixed bag approach.

The hope of those who still see American trade unions as the organizational base for securing democracy in both workplace and nation is what this book explores in its remaining chapters. The decade of the '70s gives promise of debate, hope, and renewal of labor—mixed bag or solidarity; two faces with increasing potential for melding into one.

2

Labor—the Movement

The labor movement is the AFL-CIO.

The AFL-CIO is the center, the direction, and the consent of affiliation granted by the great majority of the national and international unions of America. In a warmer sense of description, it is the House of Labor in the United States.

We cannot say that only those unions that bear the AFL-CIO tag are the movement. No trade union leader would say that. The great independent unions, which most of us in the labor movement feel should be directly affiliated with the AFL-CIO, are still part of what we know as organized labor. They may not pay monthly per capita, which is the revenue allocated from local union dues to higher union headquarters. (This per capita is only ten cents per month per member to the AFL-CIO.) The independents have purposes and practices that relate to the common ground on which all unions operate. They are certainly part of what the American labor movement is.

The Official and the Unofficial

The union member who stops long enough to think about it wants to belong to the trade union movement. Stop one and talk to him away from the workplace. Ask the member what union he belongs to and he will probably answer with a number, such as "I belong to number five."

Press the member further with, "Local 5 of what union?" If he knows you are a union leader asking the question (and I've asked it many times), his answer most likely will be, "AFL-CIO."

Now, he has seven out of nine chances to be right in his assertion. But sometimes it turns out that he just thinks he belongs to the AFL-CIO—he really belongs to an independent union like UAW, Teamsters, or UMWA.

Even more strangely, in about three out of ten instances, he doesn't turn up the answer of the union that has chartered Local 5. At least, he is not precisely correct about the name.

That leads to other questions and understandings.

The member seems to feel that all unions are organized together at some point. Thus, "AFL-CIO' is good enough for him. The chances are that he hasn't been to a regular union meeting in a long time, if at all. The member doesn't realize that perhaps over 100 international unions in the nation also have a Local 5—not just his union. And it goes on.

Unofficially, in the mind of the worker who pays union dues, he knows that he belongs to a local union. He knows that the local union is part of the union movement. He often understands little about his own local union and even less about the movement that he visualizes. He also knows that AFL-CIO is a general term in common parlance and in the media. Certainly, he thinks, he belongs to the AFL-CIO.

If he likes his job, understands that the conditions of his union contract provide him some job security and benefits that he might not otherwise have, and is not critical of the union dues deducted from one of his paychecks each month, then he might think kindly of the AFL-CIO.

He often attributes these benefits to the movement—benefits that the "clout" of an independent, local union might not have won. He also feels that it is the power of the union (movement) that requires the employer to respond more favorably to the "union demands."

But again, it may be an error to generalize.

Apprenticeable Crafts Identify More Readily

The craft union member, who has gone through an apprenticeship before he gets the journeyman's scale and conditions of work, invariably knows the "name, rank, and serial number" of almost everything about his union. He is mainly interested in his own union. The movement is incidental; it doesn't really matter to him whether or not his union is an affiliiate of the AFL-CIO.

The skilled craftsman who works in a basic industrial plant, has served apprenticeship in that plant, and belongs to an industrial union, identifies on a somewhat lesser scale with his local union than the craftsman in the single-craft type of building or in the printing trades. He also seems generally more aware of the relationship of his union to the movement.

If there is a reason for this, it relates to the fact that he intermingles in both plant and union hall with a more cosmopolitan body of workers. *Cosmopolitan* here is defined in terms of a broader range of skills, earning power, and ethnic and national backgrounds. There is less likelihood when this kind of worker mix prevails to tell someone that he and his skill can stand separate from all the rest of the workers. There seems to be a basic understanding in this community of industrial workers that they not only can stand together but "damn well better."

At best, though, the identification with the movement, official or unofficial, is secondary to the identification of the worker with his job, first, and next, his own union.

THE MOVEMENT—OFFICIAL

The very fact that the AFL-CIO exists and that it did replace two highly competitive and somewhat adversary-oriented labor movements is proof that all but a few trade union leaders recognized that "we have to hang together."

If "hang together" it is, it's easier to be together on a continuing basis than to wait for the occasion that demands unified action. Otherwise, the moments of crisis might come too often, demanding one organizational structure after another.

The AFL-CIO is a structure that loosely embraces all of the good purposes for being together. Like the ill-fated League of Nations and the existing United Nations, however, the autonomy of each of the affiliated bodies overrides the opportunity to fulfill the dream that there could be a labor movement first—then divisions within that movement based on job classifications or industry.

AFL-CIO: Official and Unexcitingly Repetitive

Official is the word for the AFL-CIO. It is the official movement. It may be neither an exciting nor an excited movement, but it is official.

If the reader is looking for excitement in the description of just what the AFL-CIO says it is and what it is all about, he is about to be disappointed. He will have to look to Chapter 7, where some of the "unofficial" members of the movement come into focus.

It is true, of course, that the press and electronic media can get the reader excited by pointing up the inconsistencies between what AFL-CIO leadership does and what its body of law sets forth as purpose. The reporting can be accurate in the process. It's the picture of leadership's gamesmanship that excites; not that of labor as an official movement.

Anti-union Americans can get worked up anytime a labor leader appears in an unpopular posture. The posture may not even be common to most labor leaders, but if one leader seems to be out of step with the mood of the times, a report of that misstep provides gleeful excitement in the anti-union countryside. In general, however, the movement operates officially in the cloth of the AFL-CIO with a certain routine that often drones rather than drives.

The AFL-CIO constantly reiterates its social, economic, and political perspectives—and it rightfully has them. The unexciting part is obvious; the times are moving faster than the official perspectives. All we have to do is to look at the AFL-CIO purposes and structure to understand why this is so—unexcitingly so in an era that has an insatiable desire for exciting responses.

What the AFL-CIO Says It Is

There was a Magna Carta. There was an American Declaration of Independence. There is the Bill of Rights asserting in ten all-embracing ways just what the American citizen is in our constitutional system.

There is the preamble to the AFL-CIO constitution, agreed to by the merger committee of the A.F. of L. and the CIO on February 9, 1955, and adopted in December, 1955.

Although these references might be differentiated by the emphasis of history, they all have equal grandeur for the body politic for which each has spoken or speaks. The merger leaders of the movement in America in 1955 stated their dreams. They were not grandiose. They were practical, although not practically spelled out. They were tinged with emotion.

But one may ask what is not emotionally flavored when dealing with the dreams—the "look-ahead" visions—of men and women who want something better for themselves and their institutions?

In a relative way, the preamble represented for most of the A.F. of L. and CIO merger leaders the direction that they wanted and believed the movement could, should—and, I presume—would take.

The preamble speaks for itself:

> The establishment of the Federation through the merger of the American Federation of Labor and the Congress of Industrial Organizations is an expression of the hopes and aspirations of the working people of America.

We seek the fulfillment of these hopes and aspirations through democratic processes within the framework of our constitutional government and consistent with our institutions and traditions.

At the collective bargaining table, in the community, in the exercise of the rights and responsibilities of citizenship, we shall responsibly serve the interests of all the American people.

We pledge ourselves to the more effective organization of working men and women; to the securing to them of full recognition and enjoyment of the rights to which they are justly entitled; to the achievement of ever higher standards of living and working conditions; to the attainment of security for all the people; to the enjoyment of the leisure which their skills make possible; and to the strengthening and extension of our way of life and the fundamental freedoms which are the basis of our democratic society.

We shall combat resolutely the forces which seek to undermine the democratic institutions of our nation and to enslave the human soul. We shall strive always to win full respect for the dignity of the human individual whom our unions serve.

With Divine guidance, grateful for the fine traditions of our past, confident of meeting the challenge of the future, we proclaim this constitution.

Implementing the Official Preamble

Thus, the preamble attributes the same level of importance to the basic labor/management process (collective bargaining), to the community, and to citizenship interests.

The preamble also expresses concern about the antifreedom forces, but not in a bill of particulars—not as the reasons for moving under duress to create labor's democracy. This negative emphasis on "enslav[ing] the human soul" precedes the positive assertion of "respect for the dignity of the human individual whom our unions serve." More poetic and less pragmatic statesmen might not have expressed their fears of totalitarian control as the reason to secure democracy in trade union halls.

Regardless of what the emphasis in the preamble meant to the union brothers who affixed their signatures to the merger agreement in 1955, they proclaimed a constitution that falls short of the purposes they sought and stated.

They call the purposes "Objects and Principles."

First among the objects is aiding workers to secure improved wages, hours, and working conditions. This is the bread and butter of the American worker. It is the heart of trade union America, even today.

This aid is tempered significantly by granting it only with "due regard for the autonomy, integrity and jurisdiction of affiliated unions." There are more than several handfuls of AFL-CIO unions that organize in one or more overlapping jurisdictions. Sometimes the "due regard" takes precedence over "aid to workers" in securing just rights.

Second among the "aid" objects is to extend "the benefits of mutual assistance and collective bargaining to workers and to promote the organization of the unorganized into unions of their own choosing for their mutual aid, protection and advancement. . . ." This is then tempered in the same statement by the "recognition to the principle that both craft and industrial unions are appropriate, equal and necessary as methods of union organization."

Tempering the Objects Essential to Merger

The tempering of object 2 was required, or all attempts at merger would have ceased. The fact that industrial unions have craft classifications and apprenticeship programs within their structures has always bothered the craft unions, which want to carve out individual craft units from the industrial total unit.

For instance, the craft electrician of the International Brotherhood of Electrical Workers (IBEW) may come out of a single craft employer unit in his early years of apprenticeship. He may find seasonal construction employment less to his liking than a journeyman's position in a year-round industrial plant or mining industry job. He becomes a part of the "total" or "industrial" union jurisdiction. He uses the same skills on his new job as on his old job. He and his union desire that he be recognized as a craft unionist—and that includes having his base union bargain for him. He tries to "carve out" through his IBEW union "intervening." His skills are appropriate to the new job. He and his craft union then contend that the craft union is "appropriate."

But the whole plant or mine might never have been organized if it had not been for the industrial union. At best, the fixed plant or mine probably had a work force that included fewer than 20 percent journeyman craft jobs.

The dispute and intervention maneuvers proceed over a period of time, often quite "inappropriately" and usually undermining the con-

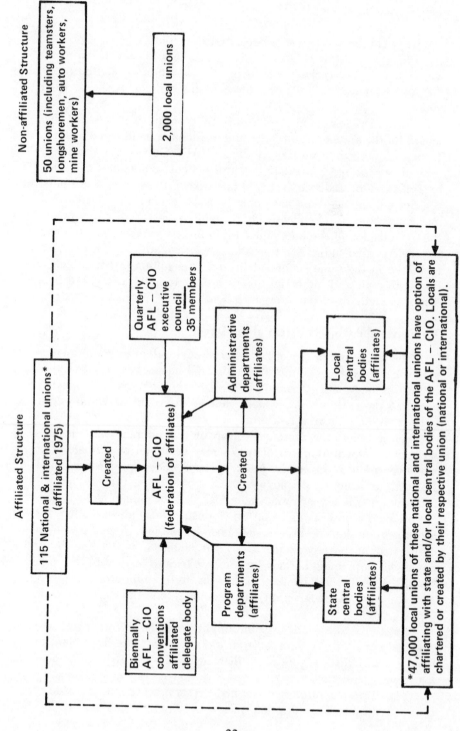

Non-affiliated Structure

50 unions (including teamsters, longshoremen, auto workers, mine workers)

2,000 local unions

Affiliated Structure

115 National & international unions* (affiliated 1975)

Created

Quarterly AFL – CIO executive council 35 members

Biennally AFL – CIO conventions affiliated delegate body

AFL – CIO (federation of affiliates)

Administrative departments (affiliates)

Program departments (affiliates)

Created

Local central bodies (affiliates)

State central bodies (affiliates)

*47,000 local unions of these national and international unions have option of affiliating with state and/or local central bodies of the AFL – CIO. Locals are chartered or created by their respective union (national or international).

cept of "mutual assistance and collective bargaining." As noted, though, if the AFL-CIO merger committee had put the period after "mutual aid, protection and advancement," merger would have stopped, too.

The official movement, the AFL-CIO, stands ready to protect autonomy and to let autonomy dispute with autonomy as front-line policy, even if "mutual assistance and collective bargaining" are not brought to workers by "organizing the unorganized."

Where the Blame Must Rest

The AFL-CIO as an institution cannot be blamed for these problems. The individual unions that "affiliate with" rather than "make up" the AFL-CIO have to be blamed. They haven't been willing to make the move away from autonomy when it comes to organizing the unorganized. This is not a movement responsibility, they say. This is the property right of each individual union in the AFL-CIO.

Thus, the AFL-CIO constitution was born to impair the bold pronouncements of both the preamble and the "Objects and Principles." This is not to say that the AFL-CIO cannot accommodate itself to taking in new jurisdictions. This is only to say it is more difficult than it should be.

The question revolves more around who is going to pay for organizing and affiliating new employee jurisdictions. Even in 1974, the AFL-CIO's revenues were only 10¢ per month for each member that any affiliate wanted to record. An affiliate identifies its members by overall numbers, not individual names. These numbers fall in the aggregate at least 10 percent short of real membership. A number of unions, including some of the largest ones, pay less than full membership. In the AFL-CIO, some call this "accepting a free ride part of the way."

Even if the AFL-CIO received 14,000,000 instead of 13,000,000 per capita units each month, the additional $100,000 would not answer the needs of organizing the unorganized. The basic $1,300,000 has no fat left in it, either.

AFL-CIO: An Underfinanced, Undermanned Movement

If any institution in the American economy is bereft of sufficient staff, it is the AFL-CIO.

"Featherbedding" is a slur term that union critics apply to what they assert is the union requirement that an employer retain more people on a job than are needed to do the job. To use this analogy, big business and government are featherbedded at management levels beyond description compared with the AFL-CIO's own staffing.

Organizing drives are not conducted by the AFL-CIO. They are conducted, if at all, by the autonomous unions—AFL-CIO affiliates and independents. If none of them wants to touch a potential jurisdiction of employment that is not organized, the AFL-CIO could do it only if it had the staff or could get its affiliate national and international unions to pool some additional funds for that purpose. In southeastern areas, in Texas, and in Los Angeles and Orange counties in California, they have.

You don't ask the hand that feeds to keep putting more feed into the trough, though. The one exception during 18 years of AFL-CIO existence was the establishment of an organizing committee for farm workers. Later, the United Farm Workers Union, built and led on a shoestring budget by Cesar Chavez, was chartered as an international union.

The AFL-CIO's contributions to the Farm Workers have been mainly through volunteer staff assistance. Even during a recent year, when up to a million dollars was paid to assist President Chavez and his stalwart members, it is not hard to determine how little this really was—less then $30 per farm worker for the year, at a time when upwards of 10,000 of the UFWU were seasonally unemployed or on the crucial picket lines of California each day. The support meant no more than food for two weeks of poverty food budgeting for each family.

Here, again, the AFL-CIO leadership represents the key affiliated national and international unions' top officers—and as George Meany so often points out, he has to represent the big international unions and satisfy them if he is to be AFL-CIO president.

Thus, it is the unions that refuse to give up their autonomy in the field of organizing—not the AFL-CIO in-house leadership that must shoulder the blame for the vast, unorganized areas of American workers.

(I must assume here that whether workers know it or not, if they can make their own voices heard at the collective bargaining table, they will improve at least their economic position with their employer. Therefore, they offer organizational potential. Since Walter Reuther's death, no one has seriously looked at most of these workers—over 50,000,000 in regular, full-time, nonmanagement jobs that are not organized in America.)

Major Potentials Remain Unorganized

To look at it another way, there are some major jurisdictions of the American work force that often inquire but for the most part remain totally unorganized because the international unions of the AFL-CIO have not provided a way for them to be organized under an AFL-CIO jurisdictional banner.

There are real estate salesmen. There are automobile salesmen. There are registered nurses. There are practical nurses. There are religious education workers. There are registered accountants. There are technicians of various professional groups. The list could go on. There is no clear-cut jurisdiction of union or unions ready to make room in the American labor movement for most of these and a hundred other job groupings.

The crafts and the industrial trades organized in the unions that existed in December, 1955, still exist. With no real expansion of their jurisdictions (only a few mergers of unions), there is a tight limitation on the "promotion of organization of the unorganized." Yet, the AFL-CIO concludes in Object 2 that this situation is "appropriate," even if it has not accomplished the goals of the constitution.

The Ten Other Objects

The objects in the AFL-CIO constitution continue:

3. To set up committees and bodies that secure affiliate, local community, and state labor input.

4. To promote full benefits for workers without discrimination (race, creed, color, etc.).

5. To secure legislation to safeguard free collective bargaining and promote the rights of "workers, farmers and consumers."

6. To protect, strengthen, preserve, and perpetuate democratic institutions and the cherished traditions of American democracy.

7. To give constructive aid to promote the cause of peace and freedom throughout the world, including cooperation with "free and democratic labor movements throughout the world."

8. To maintain the integrity of each affiliated union to the end that each affiliate shall respect and refrain from "raiding" the "established bargaining relationship" of any other affiliate, together with encouraging the elimination of conflicting and duplicating organization (but without harming the organizing jurisdicton of each affiliate).

9. To aid and encourage the sale and use of union-made goods and services and to promote the labor press and other means to further the "education of the labor movement."

10. To protect the labor movement from any and all corrupt influences and from the "undermining efforts of communist agencies."

11. To safeguard the democratic character of the labor movement and to protect the autonomy of each affiliated national and international union.

12. "While preserving the independence of the labor movement from political control," to encourage workers to register, vote, and exercise full responsibilities and rights of citizenship and political life.

I see, as do many other trade unionists, these foregoing objects as worthy. I also note that more words and attention are devoted to any object where the questions of autonomy and established bargaining relationships come into focus. These are the areas that impede rather than contribute to the organizing of the unorganized.

Whether it be union services, union goods, general labor education, or political understanding and communication, it all takes more money than the national and international union affiliates have given or will give to the AFL-CIO. As the official movement, the AFL-CIO is not designed either to organize or to educate organized or unorganized workers except in limited capacity and ways. The structure that follows the preamble and the objects and principles needs major revision if the preamble, objects, and principles are to become living reality.

THE MOVEMENT—UNOFFICIAL

Any organization that can rightfully call itself a trade union is an unofficial member of the American trade union movement.

Employee associations and so-called professional associations are sometimes referred to as unions. They really are not, although they are referred to as unions when they start to act as some people believe unions act. For instance, if the employee association "blasts" the employer by a public utterance, it is labeled a union. It may not even seek to bargain. But somebody puts the tag on the militancy and calls the association a union because it sounds like one.

Some associations, like the "not-quite-so-sure whether it is a union or a collection of professional educators" National Education Association (NEA), have begun to structure themselves like unions. They drop management members (superintendents, college deans, school principals) and seek to bargain. They threaten to and they do strike. Although they are rightfully called unions, these associations still do not think of themselves as belonging to the family of labor.

They resist official affiliation. They see no connection. They will probably get over it someday.

For the moment, we all have to understand that so-called white-collar professionals who have not joined an employee organization that identifies with trade unionism by affiliation do not quite see themselves as part of the labor movement.

They may decide that their only salvation is to strike; in the process, though, they may fail to see that the strike followed a failure to resolve a dispute at the bargaining table; in turn, they may not see collective bargaining as an exclusively trade union practice.

To me, what they are really saying is that they have a certain amount of false dignity. Some people call it snobbery. They'll get over it so long as they continue to deal with their employers by collective processes that include written agreements and the use of the strike when the chips are down. But these persons and their employee associations have simply not crossed the bridge to the movement side of the stream.

The Key Independent Unions: Their Movement Status

The independent trade unions—particularly the Teamsters, UAW, UMWA, and ILWU—have been referred to earlier.

What identifies the common ground on which national and international unions inside and outside the AFL-CIO affiliate structure meet as a movement?

The focus is on union security, primarily the ability of the union to agree in writing with an employer on the absence of the open shop. In an open shop, the union, as the collective bargaining representative for all employees in a defined unit, has no way of requiring the employees that it represents to belong as members or to pay a service (agency) fee. The purpose of either membership dues or an agency shop fee is to support the union that enforces the agreement with the employer in the interest of all employees whose working conditions are covered by that agreement.

An open shop more often than not is the downfall of the union at the local level. Any employee can take advantage of what the union can bargain for him and not pay one penny to help that union survive. A union needs income to employ full-time agents or representatives. These representatives may be elected officers of the union; they may be staff that the elected officers and board of the union employ.

The employer has full-time personnel and industrial relations staff looking after his interests in maintaining a stable, productive work force. If the union cannot afford anyone to handle the servicing of the contract provisions on behalf of the workers, the union is going to lose out over the long haul. Each time the union in this situation returns to the bargaining table, its position is weakened. The employer knows it and drives a harder bargain, whether just or unjust.

The employer also knows that an open shop means that employees will be more likely to cross a picket line if the union members vote to strike. Such company scabs, as the union would describe them, either break the strike at an early date or keep the employer in production while the strike is prolonged and the union's resources are depleted. A local union has difficulty recovering in such circumstances, even if a further open shop contract is signed with the employer.

All Unions Join to Fight "Right to Work"

The open shop draws all trade unions together to tackle a common foe.

The best example of this is in the states with so-called right to work (RTW) laws. This misnomer guarantees work to no one—employed or unemployed. RTW simply means that the state has written into its statutes or its constitution a provision known as the "compulsory open shop"—in other words, no requirement can be written into a contract between management and labor that requires an employee, even after a reasonable period of employment, to join the union that represents him in a bargaining unit.

The right to work label sounds hopeful, seeming to say that everyone in the work force is entitled to work—to a job. That wasn't how the term established its trademark in the field, however. Apparently the first time it was popularized was by Cecil B. De Mille, the motion picture director. De Mille, who was the host of the Lux Radio Theatre, refused to pay an assessment to the union under contract with the broadcaster. Though De Mille was a member of the union—the American Federation of Radio Artists—he objected to paying a one-dollar assessment the union levied on its members to use in a campaign against a proposed open shop law in California. He refused to pay the dollar and was "denied my right to work."

The advocates of compulsory open shop like the Goldwater stores and interests in Arizona and many other businesses, especially throughout the southern states, seized upon the "right to work" term that De Mille had used as the substitute for the less attractive "compulsory open shop." They were able to push the proposition through many state legislatures as well as carrying successful state constitutional referenda. Thus, the compulsory open shop has come to be known as the "right to work."

RTW does not say what some people might mistakenly take it to say: namely, the right of every person in the labor force to have a job and to work. RTW is a deceptive slogan; a dishonest description of what it is.

Every trade union leader in America—probably without exception at any level of the movement—does not want the compulsory open shop thrust upon any state that now permits unions and businesses to bargain for a union shop or modified union shop. (The requirement that on or after at least 30 days of employment, the worker shall tender his monthly dues to the local union as a condition of his continuing employment is called a "union shop." There are 31 states where laws or absence of laws permit union shop agreements.)

By the same token, every trade union leader would like to mount the 19 separate efforts needed to repeal the RTW laws in the states that have them. Trade unionists are part of the movement in this regard. They know that they cannot separate from other trade unionists and expect to win either battle: (1) the resistance against a compulsory open shop law where it is not now required, or (2) the repeal of the compulsory open shop statute where it is now required.

The movement's rallying cry is around the symbol of 14(b), the section of the National Labor Relations Act that was incorporated in a series of amendments known as Taft-Hartley in 1947. This section provides that if a state statute is restrictive in the kind of union security (membership requirement) that is permitted in a labor/management agreement, such restriction becomes a part of the National Labor Relations Act (NLRA) in that state.

On that basis, states began to enact compulsory open shop laws very rapidly in the period following 1947.

Most businesses are described in the NLRA as employers under federal law. Since most states do not have statutes with restrictions on bargaining for required union membership, approximately 90 percent of the employees in the private sector work for businesses under the jurisdiction of NLRA. They can belong to unions which are permitted to negotiate union security with employers in such a state.

Taft-Hartley abolishes the closed shop, which is a union hiring hall operating under a union-management agreement requiring that the employer first call the union to provide a worker needed to fill a job that is vacant. Taft-Hartley also restricts the union shop, which is the right of the employer to hire any person he wishes without regard to the union bargaining agent. The restriction is that the agreement between union and management cannot require that anyone employed by management in the bargaining unit belong to the union prior to the thirty-first day of employment.

Big RTW Push Stymied in 1958

All trade unions act as one on the RTW issue.

The last big effort to get the compulsory open shop into the con- stitutions of respective states was in 1958. In that year, the National Right to Work Committee initiated state committees and petition drives to place the matter on the general election ballots in Washing- ton, California, Idaho, Colorado, Kansas, and Ohio. The petition drives were successful in all six states; in all but Kansas, however, the voters rejected the compulsory open shop. In Kansas and Idaho, both pre- dominantly agricultural states, the votes were close. In the other four states, the margins against the open shop ran from 3-to-2 to 2-to-1.

In 1964, a similar ballot campaign was mounted in Oklahoma. By a narow margin, with a significant vote from rural, black, and Indian electors against the proposal, Oklahomans rejected the compulsory open shop in what was described by the trade unionists as a "surprise come-from-behind victory."

In every one of these instances, labor was united. It became a movement. Trade unionists even came from other states to talk to the union members in the states marked as targets. The unity and move- ment status aided the more progressive candidates for Congress and for the respective state legislatures. The combination of defeating RTW while electing generally pro-trade union legislators in greater proportions helped to set back the national RTW effort.

The movement understood and still understands the story. The need to keep the possibility of a modified or full union shop available for any local union to bargain with an employer is evident to all unionists. The movement's position is clear; you can't have a union shop unless an employer agrees; but he won't agree if the process is not free of governmental influence, control, or restriction. Through this free process, approximately 80 percent of all union members in the 31 states that permit the union shop are working under agree- ments with some modification of the union shop or the full union shop.

Unity in Politics and Picket Lines

The movement, unofficially, stands together on other occasions too.

Most of these occasions relate to general election politics. When a clearly pro-union political candidate is matched against a clearly anti-union candidate, the unions in any given state usually plan together on ways to help the pro-union candidate. Sometimes this public political unity is quite formally agreed upon—by separate meetings of the independents and the AFL-CIO locals, followed by a joint meeting of representatives of all unions.

Usually, the other genuine area of agreement within the movement is on the picket line. A picket tells a story—the employer is not fair to the union. The movement pulls together, and no real trade unionist from any jurisdiction crosses that picket line.

This is not a matter of, "That picket represents somebody else's union—not mine. I'll do what I want to."

This is a matter of, "That picket means that the union people in that establishment have been unable to get a fair settlement of the dispute. If it were my picket, his people would respect it. I respect his picket."

This is the labor movement at its best—a voluntary decision that is almost universally recognized by the movement, however unofficially.

Officially or unofficially, however, the structure of American trade unions emphasizes autonomy above united union action. There are reasons, both good and bad, for this situation. Without some areas of exclusive authority in which union members, not just leaders, have a way to give their own legitimate consent for a program of action, labor in America remains weaker as a movement than it needs to be. The American tradition of federalism contemplates a more responsive and viable structure than what labor in America has provided for itself.

This book looks to the future; that is where labor as a movement could and should look.

3

Labor—the Bargainer

There would be no labor movement without the bargaining table. There are unions that do not bargain. Nevertheless, without the instruments that workers use when they elect to use the union vehicle, there would be neither unions nor movement. The key instrument is the right to bargain.

The Thread That Ties

Workers in America made no real progress until the passage of the National Labor Relations Act. Segments of workers did, but most did not. The NLRA validated the thread that binds organized workers together—the right to bargain collectively with one's employer. It was Senator Robert Wagner, Democrat from New York, who moved in the early days of the New Deal to write into law the public limits and the private rights of workers to organize and to bargain.

Two years after Franklin Delano Roosevelt went to the White House, in 1935, NLRA became law.

It was more than just tradition that gave the act its identification as the Wagner Act. The venerable pro-worker senator from New York was more than just a political leader responding to the best organized union city in the nation—the heart of his constituency. Enough has been written on why Wagner became the patron political saint of America's working class. He clearly believed that the absence of a national law meant that many courts would continue to label the organization of a workplace as a conspiracy in restraint of trade. He viewed workers' rights as superior to the property rights of business. He saw both business and workers profiting from the bargaining table.

Not everyone viewed the bargaining table as being a profitable venture for the employer as well as the worker. This was especially true of most corporation executives. America was rich in resources, human as well as natural. Many business leaders and financiers had grown up in an era that "exploited the natural" and "bossed the human" resources. It was as if they had a God-given right to do so.

These men supposedly enjoyed the spoils of the system, pointing out the risks that they were taking as if these portrayed great sacrifices on their part. Resources were wasted. All too often, workers were treated as economic pawns and as human nothings.

The Wagner Wisdom: Legalize Bargaining

Wagner's political philosophy was to mix humanism and economics in the same crucible. Although FDR, as President, received the public credit, it was Wagner who carried the battle for a public law legalizing a union's right to bargain. If FDR had seen as clearly as Wagner NLRA's economic impact on the nation, he might have proposed the act himself as rapidly as he put a moratorium on the banks in 1933. NLRA might even have preceded or paralleled the NRA–WPA–PWA–NYA–CCC economic alphabets of governmental economic spoon-feedings.

Wagner perceived that the dignity of workers as individuals rested on their ability to select their own spokesmen. In terms of the New Deal economics required to lift the nation out of its most severe depression, he saw the bargaining table as a way of sharing more equitably the fruits of American business—particularly basic industry and larger business endeavors. He never ceased to point out that if the bargaining table brought significant increases in wages, the workers would spend most of their earnings in the marketplace for consumer goods. Who profiteth most? That was Wagner's question to the former corporate attorney, the President of the United States.

Finally, the point was made—as the worker profits, so does the business that produces and the business that distributes the material wealth that America had become famous for producing. In 1935, five months after the midterm congressional elections, the Wagner Act finally reached the President's desk for signature. The upturn that marked the next two years of the New Deal related almost directly to the Wagner Act. The upturn was even more striking than the first two years of the Roosevelt administration.

Industrial Unionization: New Bargaining Arenas

The Wagner Act gave credence and birth to industrial unionization in America. It also gave the largest of the building craft unions a chance to reexamine their own processes of dealing with the construction and heavy maintenance contractors. Many of these unions had been around for years, had struck employers when they were strong enough to do so, and had reached agreements primarily on wages. But the building trades had been hampered by the legal entanglements they had often faced before the governmental third house—the judiciary. They had not been signing contracts; they had not been writing their agreements bilaterally.

So the craft unions—particularly in printing and construction areas—were clearly given a new ball park, the opportunity to take on new players, and the ability to reduce their big plays to writing between the contestants—their employers and their members.

But the economic boon to the working people in America was more clearly demonstrated in the big fixed plant industries. He who has nothing and suddenly has something finds his circumstances more than substantially improved. The unskilled workers, the semiskilled workers, and even the skilled trades within the basic industrial plants of America began to find infinite improvement at the bargaining table. They found release from the abject poverty that proclaimed ownership of their souls at the company store.

Thus, the sit-downs began to be replaced by the full-scale process of bargaining, by the legally recognized picket lines outside the plant gates, by the signing of contracts. It was primarily the Wagner Act—the NLRA—that made this possible.

The legal battles over the act's constitutionality did not slow either the signing of the agreements or the burgeoning growth of industrial unions. Before America entered the Second World War, the court decisions had been made and the basic industrial plants had been organized.

CIO—Movement of Basic Industrial Bargainers

Industries like steel, auto, rubber, textiles, electrical goods, paper, packing—just to name a few—had most major production facilities under union contract. As business began to boom, workers shared decently if not luxuriously in the benefits of the bargaining table. Collective bargaining started a new movement, the Congress of Industrial Organizations; at the same time, the older American Federation of Labor found its basically craft-oriented union structure ready to expand.

This meant competition between the industrial and craft segments in the workplace. Had it not been for the national emergency of a world war, the competition between the unions and the two labor federations would have become more vigorous and occasionally strife-filled in the early '40s.

In the postwar era of adjustment, union shop agreements that had been secured by steady membership from the defense industrial giants meant that both A.F. of L. and CIO unions were generally in positions to maintain their strength at the respective bargaining tables.

The returned-from-the-war work force was more interested in job markets than in any philosophical attachment to a labor movement. This work force was generally young and had not been among the militants who had built the union movement of the late '30s. They had economic and job adjustments in common with the older work force, but they did not share their elders' understanding of the bargaining table, the battle to establish union rights, and the requirement to join in the membership of the union.

The politicians took advantage of this transitional period—especially when fewer persons than expected turned out at the polls in off-year 1946—and the two movements of labor in America were unsuccessful in staving off amendments to NLRA in 1947. Those amendments survived the veto of President Truman, who had not forgotten the economic mess of 1929–1935. But Senator Robert Taft and Congressman Fred Hartley, the sponsors of the amendments, held their ground.

Taft-Hartley: A Turnaround for Unions

The NLRA has subsequently been referred to as Taft-Hartley because of the basic objections that labor leadership had toward major provisions that are still in effect—almost three decades later.

Taft-Hartley was a turnaround; unlike the Norris-LaGuardia Act of 1927 and the Wagner Act of 1935, Taft-Hartley "equalized" against the expanding union movement and "protected" big business.

It added and defined unfair labor practices; it reinstituted court injunctions (although only for use by the government); it provided for penalties if unions either violated contract provisions or failed to file their governing constitutions and financial reports with the government; it prohibited union contributions to campaigns for federal office; it outlawed jurisdictional strikes and secondary boycotts; and it required union officers to sign noncommunist affidavits. This latter provision, accepted for a variety of reasons by even the liberal garment trade A.F. of L. leaders, caused the second and final disaffiliation of the United Mine Workers, as John L. Lewis berated any labor leader who would dare stand for this "hateful, despicable Act contrary to our concept of American privileges . . . [which] . . . makes second-class citizens out of every man around the [A.F. of L.] Council table and every man he represents."

Taft-Hartley's Effect on Bargaining

Taft-Hartley did not specifically alter the bargaining process, but indirectly it had major effects upon it.

For instance, 14(b) permitted open shops by state laws, whereupon the states of the Old South marched into the compulsory open shop camp in just a few years; the Western Plains and Mountain states also came under real pressure, and a number lost the union shop privilege in campaigns that were always well financed.

Indiana had RTW but turned it around; Louisiana had RTW and still does in part, but its construction and basic industrial and transportation economic segments can now bargain for a union shop. Outside of those two instances, the southern states and Iowa, Kansas, the Dakotas, Wyoming, Utah, Nevada, and Arizona are saddled with bargaining that proclaims nothing about union security, the right of the majority of the bargaining unit to sign with management the requirement that all employees shall join.

Agency shops have appeared with increasing frequency in these states and still stand wherever court proceedings have not put them aside. Usually, the agency shop is bargained with employers who have union shops in their branches in other states. An agency shop requires in lieu of worker membership the payment of a fee to cover all the union costs of bargaining and administering the union's responsibility under the bargained agreement—usually slightly less than the monthly dues.

Additionally, Taft-Hartley has brought more determination and success on the management side of the bargaining table to include restrictive provisions in the contract itself. One of the most harassing of these from any local union's point of view is the requirement that a picket line of another union shall not be respected even if that union also has a legitimate bargaining unit with the same employer. This requirement is based on Taft-Hartley conditions that provide that no union officer can instruct the union members not to cross a picket line.

The clincher at the bargaining table puts an additional legal liability on the employee who refuses to cross a picket line of another union at his place of employment. No union officer needs to be involved in that case. The contract nails it shut on the union member. The bargaining table, weakened by Taft-Hartley from the union point of view, forces the union member to take on the appearance, if not the fact, of being a scab, a worker who is willing to cross a picket line for the purpose of working for an employer who is being struck.

Union Shops Are a Stronger Threat to Management

A union that is 100 percent organized and has every potential member in a bargaining unit in dues-paying status represents a stronger threat against an employer when impasse comes to the bargaining table. Taft-Hartley effectively weakens this threat in the 19 states noted earlier.

The RTW states have generally lagged behind comparable union shop states except for Nevada, in both hourly wages paid in nonfarm industries and in per capita income—where legalized gambling attracts big money and creates an artificial situation that is not comparable in terms of the economy of an average state. Then, too, the plain fact is that the big service trades unions, the entertainers' and performers' unions, and the building trades all sign agency shop contracts in the principal areas of population—Las Vegas, Reno, Lake Tahoe.

Perhaps this point illustrates something else about the bargaining table. Where workers are in demand by the public—in this instance, the great stars of stage, screen, and television—they have set standards that must be met in all areas of the nation where they work. Their bargaining table is not exclusively in Las Vegas. If they appear in Nevada, the conditions of contract are clear.

What does this mean to the other workers around the entertainment and gambling casinos of Nevada? The picket line means something—that's what it means. In Las Vegas, for example, the Hotel and Restaurant and Bartenders International Union (Culinary Workers, as they call themselves) have a contract covering one of their largest local unions in the nation—upwards of 16,000 persons working on any one day.

If the Culinary Workers put up a picket line, the entertainers do not appear. If the American Federation of Musicians or any of the unions in the Associated Actors and Artistes of America (Actors' Equity, AFTRA—television and radio artists, Guild of Musical Artists, Guild of Variety Artists, Screen Actors Guild, or Screen Extras Guild) puts up a picket line, the possibility is almost total that the maids won't be making up the rooms and the food and drinks won't be on the customers' tables.

One union thus provides a bulwark of strength to the other in Nevada with two obvious results: (1) the working people in almost all categories, including public workers, have shared more readily in the higher income available and have had their seasonal layoffs shored up through union contracts; (2) the consuming public has been willing to pay the prices that the business entrepreneurs have set on their services because they come to Nevada with the illusive hope that they may find the price refunded at the gaming table. But without the bargaining table for the workers, there would be no sharing of the profits of the gaming tables provided for the customers.

No one should overlook either the huge stake that the federal government has in employment in the atomic installations in the desert and the great reclamation projects or the huge copper industry in the state. The miners in the copper pits of the Mountain states are 100 percent organized for economic protection and safety on the job, compulsory open shop notwithstanding, and more and more federal employees are bargaining for everything but wage levels.

Copper is a big industry, controlled by a handful of major corporations. The tough, physically demanding, often dangerous work of mining in America has demanded strong unions. If any miner in the U.S. has exercised this common sense judgment almost all the way, it is the worker in the great open pits of copper in the west, including RTW States like Nevada, Utah, and Arizona.

The other 49 states are not comparable to Nevada in terms of the mutual support that one bargaining unit gives to another. They vary as much as do the business operations and the union structures. Urban areas within the same state even vary one from the other.

When we talk about strong union centers, we are really talking about the bargaining tables within those urban areas. We are not necessarily talking about the totality of labor as a movement in that area—although sometimes the strong bargaining centers are by coincidence also effective as a movement.

Bargaining Table Gains Are Clear; Movement Gains Less Clear

Movement gains are not easy to substantiate; union leaders find them much easier to proclaim. Sometimes the proclamations are hollow, even to the sensitive and alert leader within the area of movement where the proclamation is made.

To expand upon the contrast in these two strengths, substantially improved working conditions and wage and health and welfare levels set by union contracts can be identified in fact. The economic benefits obtained in a contract may not be precisely proclaimed in the media, but the local businessman finds the workers to be better spenders; the workers find themselves more certain of their status, and they proceed to distribute their earnings in the marketplace, not only with

economic surety, but with personal confidence that bespeaks job security as found in that bargained contract. Thus, the community and
the worker can identify the bargaining process and its benefits.

The movement's strength, however, relates to the manner in
which the trade unions that do bargain in the community get their
members to act together and in the common interest. Let me give
some examples—some that identify and some that do not identify
whether or not the movement has strength.

The grape boycott against A & P and Safeway supermarkets in
America in the late '60s and again in the '70s has been effective. Trade
unionists of all jurisdictions have ceased to buy table grapes. This is
about the only way they can show a recognition of the facts that the
Farm Workers are now a union and that stoop laborers in the fields of
America are still disadvantaged in many ways: earning power, opportunities for personal health care, decent housing, and education for
their children.

This point is given a special twist when it is noted that the
Teamsters do not belong to the AFL-CIO family of labor and so have
permitted themselves to be drawn into a position of aiding the growers by signing alternative contracts even when they do not have the
workers' consent.

The Teamsters argue that their contracts provide clauses that are
equal to or better than the newly organized United Farm Workers
Union, AFL-CIO. The catch is that the contracts have generally been
signed without the consent of the workers. In some cases, these contracts cover no members, being only for the convenience of the growers, who are often interlocked with warehousing, distribution, and
processing businesses whose employees are, in fact, Teamsters.

Thus, the contracts stand to impede the labor movement's support
of a union that does have members and is trying to get to the growers'
bargaining table with legitimate demands.

Within the movement, from the membership hall to George
Meany's office, the Teamsters' actions have been labeled as both
union-breaking and sweetheart argeements (those signed for the convenience of the employer rather than the benefit of the employer's
workers).

Movement Aids Farm Workers' Boycotts

In spite of this, the movement can contend that it has strength,
particularly in the larger urban centers, where chain stores have re-
ported major reductions in sales of table grapes and even other items
of fresh produce. Where the recent boycotts of table grapes and ice-

berg lettuce have resulted in a decline in fresh produce purchases ex-
ceeding 25 percent, the movement does indeed exhibit strength.

This is a direct and understandable labor issue—boycott of a
product that is not union handled or processed. It means to the trade
unionist that a commercial interest is blocking the right of a worker
in another area to organize in the union of his choice and bargain a
contract that covers the fruits of his labor. Thus, the movement stands
to be more successful here. This example has additional overtones,
though. When Senator Wagner succeeded in passing NLRA, he did so
only by agreeing to a compromise that deleted from the definition of
workers and employers covered by the act those in the "agricultural
and domestic" areas.

Thus, when the Taft-Hartley amendments were tacked onto
NLRA, the farm workers were not covered under the restrictions on
the secondary boycott. The unions in nonagricultural pursuits are. By
the same token, the farm workers do not have a statutory procedure
to file for a representation election under federal law; therefore,
NLRA is of no help in certifying the UFWU, the Teamsters, the Meat
Cutters and Butcher Workmen, or any other union that has attempted
to organize any workers in the fields, orchards, and vineyards of
America.

To put it another way, the Farm Workers can boycott the retail
supermarket even though they do not seek a contract to cover any of
its workers. The Retail Clerks and the Meat Cutters, who have contracts with the supermarket, cannot boycott the growers as a means
of bringing pressure on supermarket chains to sign a better working
agreement covering their members. If they acted to stop work by
picketing any other employer that supplies products or services for
the supermarket to sell, the Clerks and Meat Cutters would be subject
to severe penalties—fines and even jail sentences. The Farm Workers
are not.

Movement as a Political Force: Not So Clear

Another aspect of the movement's strength is in the political
arena. Of course, no one disputes the assertion that a union leader
does not control the votes of the union members or of their families.
But sometimes the movement at one level or another proclaims that
political victories have been won because of their vocal support, their
precinct organizational support, and/or their official endorsements.

It is debatable whether or not the movement exhibits this strength
by actually holding the balance of power in electing members to Congress, to state legislatures, or to local governing bodies and boards of

education. But the movement often proclaims its strength when its endorsed candidates win.

Trends, the support of others in the community, the organization of political parties, the personal appeal of the candidates, and other factors have to be put into the analysis in each case. Little valid research has really been set forth on just what labor's role as a movement has been in terms of community or political strength. By assertion, especially in industrial centers, labor has done well. By assertion or not, labor has done less well where 20 percent or fewer of the working people belong to unions.

Measure of Strength: Bargaining Table

It all comes back to the basics—the bargaining table is a better measurement of strength. The heavily industrialized urban center is the key to labor strength in America.

Except when politicians and union leaders themselves get out of step with what the people perceive as the proper course, there is a less evident way to judge labor's strength. Labor's bosses in the political arena might be judged: "Labor did not have the strength it claimed." But I would temper that judgment by saying that labor leaders, like all human beings, err from time to time. Political losses suffered by labor candidates can more often than not be written off as errors in leadership judgment prior to the campaign.

Down under, the union member and his family have spoken as if they have no relationship to the political inclinations of their leaders. But at the bargaining table, these same members might well support the same leaders because the bargaining table's strength is well defined to all—the union leader, the bargainer for the employer, the workers, and the community. The first three see the contract for what it is. The community sees the workers distribute the economic benefits of collective bargaining among the businesses and the community projects that warrant support. The bargaining table is thus more clearly defined, whereas labor's effectiveness in the political community is dim and often blurred.

DIFFERENCES IN BARGAINING PATTERNS

Bargaining patterns are determined on both sides of the bargaining table. These patterns depend upon a multitude of factors.

The purpose is to establish union security and gain benefits for workers on labor's side. Management's objective is to get a contract that will ensure as much stability in the work force as possible while continuing stockholders' earnings, in the private sector, and service and satisfaction to the citizens in the public sector.

If all this sounds elementary, we can at least reduce bargaining to its simplest common ground in every case. The union, on behalf of the workers in the bargaining unit, and management, on behalf of the stockholders, seek to reach an agreement that will govern the defined conditions of work for a defined period of time.

The common ground, then, is to reach agreement, sign the agreement, and live with the agreement.

A Multitude of Factors

Whatever the agreement is to be, it still depends upon a multitude of factors.

Does the employer bargain for himself or does he join a combine of employers who use the same staff services through a common organization established for the purpose of bargaining (if not counseling on all matters relating to the employer's labor relations)? Thus, factor number one is employer associations, employer councils, or as I prefer to call them, employer combines.

If the attitude, philosophy, and operating technique of such employer combines is to ward off unions, then bargaining is often approached as a hostile process. Some people would tone down this description of the combine's purpose from one of being hostile to one of simply being an adversary.

Supposedly, the employer council type of professional industrial relations exists either because some employers are too small to employ expert staff on their own or because large employers hope that detaching themselves from the negotiating process as much as possible makes it easier for them to drive a harder bargain. The same is true on the union side—the business agent or chief negotiator ought not to be on the employer's payroll. In either case, both parties at the bargaining table are less personally involved in the outcome and cannot be blamed for trying to drive a harder bargain.

Combine Bargaining: Union Reaction

The employer combine approach often leads to fears by the union that the employer is trying to break the union. If there is anything that distrubs union leaders, in particular, and union rank and file, generally, it is the threat to destroy the bargaining unit, if not the union itself. This is how the greater number of the employer associations/councils/combines are viewed. "Keep away" is usually the union's battle cry. The union negotiators would much rather negotiate directly with the employer himself.

The employer combine has a bearing on the bargaining process. It provides the research, negotiating, and legal staff services that smaller unions have a hard time matching. When you get outside your own league, it's harder to win the match. And when you don't win, the workers in the unit are just as likely to desert the union as the fans are a losing team. This is what the employer often wants; the employer combine provides him that opportunity at considerably less cost than he would have incurred by hiring his own professionals; and if he protects his wage and working conditions costs against the union that is recognized to bargain with him, he may not have to face that union very long.

In thousands of businesses, unions have sought to be the employees' bargaining agent; many actually have gained this status; but many first rounds are often failures to the union that has just won the bargaining right. No employer wants to call this kind of bargaining union breaking, but it is what he has sought and thus it is, in fact, just that. This is one of the multitude of outcomes in the bargaining process.

As the employer continues with the same combine for the second and succeeding rounds of bargaining, the purpose often exhibited by the employers' group is to keep all agreements pretty much in line; to keep workers' gains minimal; to make it clear to each union that the employer can't give away much without infuriating all other employers in the combine. The combine stresses that there really isn't anything to expect but minimal gains.

With all due respect to one of the largest employer combines in the country, the Mountain States Employers Council serving a large segment of business interests in the Plains and Mountain states, the sophistication of experience has mellowed some of its concepts of the labor-management relationship.

This council provides employer counsel on all aspects of personnel relations. It assumes that each member of the professional staff who serves a business member dealing with a union has the competency to set his own style and pace. Accordingly, Mountain States Employers Council has no standard pattern of how to deal with a union—whether that union is in the organizational stage or has many years of experience at the bargaining table. The professional staff member has the opportunity to adapt himself to the character of the employer rather than following a standard operating procedure. MSEC has found the practice productive.

Likewise, in many instances, unions are getting less and less critical of meeting the MSEC negotiator rather than the employer's own industrial relations expert. Unions often find that the MSEC staffer is no longer in the business of being tough about unions, egging the employer into a strike on the assumption that the union can be weakened or broken, or adopting a program designed to keep the union far away from the employer's door.

If this practice is followed more in the future by employer combines, a new maturity may be on the horizon for labor and management.

Strikes and Other Impairments

A negative attitude often provokes strikes. When the strike begins, the employers' group usually withdraws what little it had earlier included in its proposal. This hardens rather than softens the conflict and fills the subsequent bargaining sessions with more highly charged emotions. Reasoned judgments are less likely to appear. Settlements are harder to find. The bargaining process is impaired.

Impairing the process is one step that usually weakens or eventually dissolves the labor-management relationship. I believe this step is usually taken consciously by employer combines. Whether or not this is so, the end result is the same. One of the arguments frequently made against this assertion is that an employer combine becomes a major business in its own right. If it successfully defeated each of the labor unions facing its employer clientele, it would do away with its own business; it would self-destruct.

The argument doesn't hold, however. The employer combine is much like the defense department of a nation. It is the on-guard establishment to orient all member clients on ways to avoid unionization of any segment of their respective work forces. It aids the employer who faces an election for union representation. It teaches the employer how to avoid the election in the first place.

If the employees choose the union in spite of the professional efforts of the combine, the staff then needs to give more than the usual service to the employer in his first round of bargaining with the newly certified union unit. There are just enough of these new certifications under governmentally supervised elections to keep the employer combine very much in business.

Even more significant, however, is the fact that the employers' group often has as members large corporate interests that seldom use the services of the combine. Whatever their purposes might be, it is logical to conclude that they view the combine for the most part as a standby resource.

There are some labor-management policy decisions that business prefers to make through this type of employer grouping rather than through the manufacturers or commerce-and-industry types of associations, which often concentrate on other areas of private-sector economic decision making. Combines self-destruct? Not a chance!

Combines Indirectly Affect the Movement

Although employer combines deal with labor basically as a bargaining agency, they also deal with it as a movement.

If the bargaining agents are generally held at bay through the expertise of the combine, the movement in the broader sense is generally less effective in its community endeavors. For one thing, each union has to devote more of its resources to maintain its own bargaining security.

If we added up all of the man-days spent at the bargaining table, we would see precisely how overoccupied the union becomes while trying to match the strategic moves of the combine staff. Often, the combine strategy of emphasizing in one way or another that its employer client will accept a strike before giving in even to the least of the proposals advanced by the union means that the union leadership turns from all other tasks to the bargaining table alone. If there is a community service fund-raising drive or a political election campaign in progress, these get little attention from the union leadership (and thus probably the membership), even though they might otherwise receive a major share of union attention.

Employer combines—groups, associations, councils—whose principal purpose is to deal with labor-management relationships have had much to do with how unions bargain, especially since Taft-Hartley. Out front or behind the scenes, these combines probably deal with almost half of the total membership of American labor in the private sector. To date, the combines have not become a significant factor in public employee bargaining. And even though their prime clients are in the service and retailing trades, they deal with broad jurisdictions of the business community—construction, heavy industry, and transportation.

HEAVY-INDUSTRY BARGAINING: STEEL AND AUTO

Since the days of the Wagner Act, the industries that supply the basic goods and tools of our society have managed rather dramatically to adjust to the process of bargaining.

For one thing, basic industry is essentially large. It has required major capital investment; it has demanded top-level executive skill; it can afford to staff industrial relations departments.

On the union side, the employee organizational potential is equally sizable. As the industrial type of union grew in the 1930s and '40s, it inevitably found spirited leadership. In the absence of an already established bureaucracy, natural talent found it easier to make its way to the front of the ranks. Leaders with some vision and daring established resourceful staff services and internal publications that moved communication in both directions—from leadership to rank and file and vice versa.

The two largest of the unions, in auto (UAW) and in steel (USWA), learned how to get the facts on the bargaining table because the leadership was more than responsive—it was often inventive.

Exterior Demands Cause Auto and Steel to Respond

National industrial patterns encouraged both parties—business and labor—to succeed at the bargaining table. There are too many pressures to expect that the auto industry can afford to shut down for too long. There are too many demands in the domestic and world markets to expect that basic steel can normally either stockpile inventories or afford to close shop for any extended period of time.

The consumer end economic demands of the total society have helped both big steel and big auto to reach agreement. But so have the techniques and programs adopted by both the UAW and the Steelworkers. Each has had its own way of doing business with the big companies, but the pattern of each industry has also had its effect on labor as bargainer.

Although the period of industrial unionization growth saw the merger or demise of many automobile manufacturers, America found itself in the '60s with more automotive models and options available than ever before. This was true even though only three giant corporations (GM, Ford, and Chrysler) and one small producer (American) were turning out American automobiles. Western Europe and Japan's highly competitive smaller auto models made inroads with the American car buyer at the same time.

In this situation, the bargaining table was both innovator and reactor.

UAW talked about and made moves in a modified way toward a guaranteed annual income. Annual model changeover periods had always taken a toll of workers' savings during seasonal layoffs. UAW is still seeking to bargain for planned production schedules to avoid layoffs. Deferred-income payments were built into new types of health and welfare plans—extended vacation periods with pay at intervals of five or ten years; early-retirement plans; higher benefits and more attractive incentives for retirement of production workers.

Without analyzing the extent to which UAW has gone and still plans to go to broaden the scope of the bargaining, suffice it to say here that health, safety, and bread-and-butter issues still dominate the bargaining table; the dream of the guaranteed annual wage and union participation in setting the price of the American automotive product is still pretty much the vision of the late Walter Reuther.

Government Funding and the Bargaining Process

UAW deals in space-age industries, too, an area of the economy where heavy government subsidy has controlled the economics of the bargaining table more than in auto. The International Association of Machinists (IAM) shares heavily with UAW in the bargaining with the basic areospace producers. Both unions have had to look further than the stock market and dividend returns in seeking fruits from the bargaining in this arena.

When government itself is a prime consumer—especially the Department of Defense and, in a more limited way, NASA and its space programs—unions have to react differently. Lockheed's need for governmental subsidies and Boeing's failure to get SST production going were severe blows to the IAM and the general consumer economy despite the Machinists' favorable contractual conditions.

The impact on just that one union had more than local ramifications in Seattle, Wichita, and Southern California. The Lockheed and Boeing situations put union and management into allied postures in the political halls of the nation. It aided in labor's acceptance of the Nixon appointment of Jim Hodgson of Lockheed as Secretary of Labor after George Shultz moved to other special and cabinet assignments. It founded some mutual political friendships in the projection of Washington Senator Henry Jackson's bid for the Democratic nomination for President.

Both management and labor spokesmen responded from the same

bargaining table as they sought congressional approval of loans for Lockheed and billions for Boeing's SST.

UAW Bargaining Other Than Auto

The UAW has also organized the heavy-equipment and agricultural-equipment manufacturing industries, a major segment of the American economy. Here, the responses that management and UAW make to each other do not necessarily parallel those in auto. Seasonal manufacturing factors are not the same; the typical American does not generally drive either the sophisticated field harvester or the earth mover; the demands of the multitude of consumers obviously are not so directly related.

However, farmers, ranchers, their local communities, the giant general construction contractors, and America's burgeoning agribusiness corporations place sufficient economic pressures on the big producers to keep the equipment rolling out of factories. John Deere, Massey, Wayne, International Harvester, McCormick Deering, Caterpillar are major corporations in areas of industrial union concern and attention.

In the long haul, what UAW can gain from these heavy industrial operators is a transferable commodity when it comes to bargaining in auto—and vice versa.

Neither union nor management has successfully sought "combine" bargaining in auto, agricultural implement, aerospace, or heavy equipment. UAW bargains with Ford, Chrysler, General Motors, and American Motors as separate entities.

Selective Bargaining

UAW uses one of the big three to try out its bargaining program at each time of contract renewal. This is not to say that passing around this selective plum (or better, "experience") among Chrysler, Ford, and General Motors automatically guarantees identical agreements with the other two, once the selected has settled.

This is not to say that the three giants in auto are not comparing notes while the "selected" is at the bargaining table. And this is not to say that selective bargaining has in recent renewal bargaining rounds ended up with a selective strike. But UAW, keeping many members at work, has found the process advantageous; the two unselected corporations in the interim are able to continue full-scale production from which they derive economic benefits, especially since the bargaining is usually at model-changeover seasons.

Since the Studebaker experience of the 1950s, when UAW accepted voluntary cutbacks in worker benefits across the board in the hope of saving Studebaker at South Bend, Indiana, UAW bargains after the fact of the big three settlements with smaller American Motors. Contract adjustments are made throughout to take account of AM's small share of the market. The Studebaker adjustments came after the contract conditions were set; the AM adjustments come at the contemporary bargaining table.

All of this generalized discussion about the largest of the American industrial unions is aimed at the point of understanding that unions, even in heavy industry, use different bargaining patterns with different employers—even if the employers are owned by conglomerate structures. We must also conclude that big national and multinational corporations do not turn their employer bargaining responsibilities over to any combine, council, or group association.

Monotony in the New Plants

The bargaining world of the UAW also illustrates a tangent of the process that is more and more apparent in American industry—especially heavy industry and electronics.

In the early part of the 1970s, the Chevrolet Motor Division of GM opened a new plant in Lordstown, Ohio, to produce its compact Vega. Approximately 7,800 production workers, most of whom were considerably younger than the median age in the established Chevrolet plants in Michigan, determined as a total unit that they didn't like everything they found in their new workplace.

In simple terms, the jobs were boring and monotonous—the same inherent problem that has faced all workers since the efficient use of machinery was swept in with the Industrial Revolution. Monotony reduces alertness; attention spans decrease; accident indices rise; injuries that seemed impossible become more prevalent; general frustration and group reactions set in.

Well-bargained contract or not, neither management nor union leadership found the work force easy to reckon with. There were strikes of the wildcat variety (initiated on the job and not part of the orderly process normally observed when negotiations fail and strike-notice deadlines have been reached).

The UAW had to agree that there were some job terms that needed changing, contract notwithstanding. Vega management found that they couldn't blame undisciplined youth in general terms. Settlements were made. A new kind of democracy, reminiscent of the sit-down days in Dearborn and at Willow Run, hit the workplace. Workers were proving to both leaderships—union and management—that they could take some matters in their own hands.

In the 1973 auto negotiations, UAW President Leonard Woodcock, intelligently responsive as he had to be, made more than one bargaining proposal and more than one public reference to the need for business to make highly automated plant jobs attractive enough to hold the attentiveness of workers. He even noted that the union had to take an interest at the bargaining table as to how assembly lines, production engineering, and job scope must be revised if workplaces are to hold competent workers. This challenge lies ahead for both sides of the bargaining table.

Steel—Continuing Bargaining

The basic industry of steel production relates to auto manufacturing, to mining (coal and iron ore and special metals like molybdenum), to air and water pollution, to growing junkyards of discarded metals and autos, and to rail transportation. Its roots are deep and basic to America as the top industrial nation of the world.

As the auto industry has Detroit, steel has a city of central focus, Pittsburgh. Unlike auto, which still has more than half of its basic production in Michigan, steel has its basic centers along the major lake shores and in the river bottom lands from Pittsburgh and Buffalo to Wheeling and Youngstown to Ashtabula and Gary to Birmingham and Pueblo to Geneva and Fontana.

Like the UAW in Detroit, the United Steelworkers of America in Pittsburgh has not moved its headquarters to Washington, D.C., as so many unions have. It has stayed in the native environment of the basic industry. Like UAW, USWA is the single union that the major producers face in covering the units of the basic steel system, known as p & m—production and maintenance.

Unlike auto, though, the big ten companies (U.S., Inland, Republic, Jones & Laughlin, Bethlehem, etc.), by mutual consent and agreement bargain as a team and accept the same master agreement. (CF & I Steel used to be the eleventh member of the team, but since it is now primarily under the ownership of the Crane Company, it has elected not to join in the master agreement bargaining.)

UAW has separate wage and working conditions policy teams for each of the four auto producers, drawn from the membership of the locals at the respective plants. USWA, by contrast, adapts itself to the industry and has a total wage and policy council, elected at the local union levels in proportion to membership and work force population. Contract approval and decision making is vested in this industry-wide union policy council, which includes members from CF & I and smaller basic steel producers. There is no U.S. Steel policy as contrasted with Bethlehem Steel policy for the USWA bargaining teams.

Steelworkers' Democracy

The USWA approach has made possible the concentration of staff resources able to look at every possible national, international, and local plant economic situation in drafting proposals for the policy council. Although it becomes so sophisticated that one can sometimes suspect that there are grumblings at the grass roots of every USWA local, there are two basic ingredients in the Steelworkers' system that seem to protect it from either abuse or membership disenchantment. Both relate to the secret ballot.

The national officers of USWA are elected by a total membership referendum—not by a convention of delegates, as in the UAW and most unions. The policy council representatives in basic steel are elected by a secret ballot in which every member in every bargaining unit at each basic steel plant across the nation may vote. Terms of office vary among the unions, three or four years being the most common.

If either the officers or the policy council representatives fail to satisfy membership, they can be reached at the next go-around in the voting booth—and they are, when the complaints crescendo faster than the plaudits. USWA President I. W. "Abe" Abel replaced the luxuriating David J. McDonald through such a grass-rooted insurgence in the 1960s.

USWA's bargaining is focused on basic steel, but it also has local unions in diverse businesses. (Many are usually near a basic steel foundry or fabricating plant.) It is in aluminum and can production. It has merged with two major union segments in the last decade—Mine, Mill and Smelter (mostly copper mining workers) and District 50, the old John L. Lewis catchall organizing committee that represented units as far removed from one another as atomic energy workers and teachers in public schools. It broke away from the United Mine Workers in an independence move that was short-lived enough for it to move back into the labor mainstream as a USWA affiliate in the early '70s.

Steelworkers' "No-Strike" Bargaining

The union's new emphasis in basic steel will be the bargaining relationship that might both succeed and breed other successes, not just in USWA bargaining units but across other major industries. The big ten of steel and USWA are testing a no-strike, no-lockout policy in the 1970s. The process has not been defined in total detail yet. It may turn out to be a new era of open-end agreements with either continuous or continuing bargaining the order of the day.

The big ten and USWA are looking at job security as well as corporate earning power in a highly competitive international market with Japanese and European interests allegedly cutting into the American steel producers' markets. If there are no strikes, there can be planned production—no stockpiling by the employers, no strike-fund building by the unions. Production ought to be markedly more efficient; workers' benefits should be kept at a reasonable and even improved pace, compared with the rest of the economy.

Here the bargainers also join hands at the political table. The militant activists in new unions sometimes look at this as an unwarranted sweetheart agreement in a union that once was viewed as socially and politically progressive. Only time will tell if the critics are even partially correct. Unions without spirit more often than not fail their members by not securing true improvements at the bargaining table. Again, time will tell.

Burke-Hartke—Protection for Workers?

Tariffs and artificial barriers used to be the concern of the politicians and the business entrepreneurs. Now, the concern has spread to the worker who finds himself unemployed because a foreign competitor has taken away part of his former employer's market, both at home and abroad.

Burke-Hartke is the early '70s push of employees at the steel bargaining table. It involves politics, for certain. It deals with protectionist philosophy.

Burke-Hartke is not exactly the dream of the modern industrialist, however. He is going multinational. He is not only seeking markets throughout the world—he is capitalizing and building plants and employing more and more workers on non-American soil.

The balance of payments problem and the mid-'70s recession have implications of world economic interdependence that present questions for both camps—the open- and the high-barrier advocates in the battle over Burke-Hartke.

The American worker, on the other hand, is not multinational. His capital is his labor. It is not distributable to many locations. The worker can invest his capial in only one spot—where he labors.

Burke-Hartke is aimed at taxing the Amercan-based multinational corporation on its foreign earnings in lieu of the corporation's investing solely in plants that can employ the American worker on American soil. Part of the theory of this bill is that the tax dollars collected from American corporate earnings outside the United States will reduce the tax on both persons and businesses at home. These dollars, then, will be put into consumer flow. Consumer demand creates production, distribution, and services that employ people. In turn, some of this domestic production will use the products of basic steel in America.

Thus, the bargaining agreements that relate to continuous production also relate to the overall economic condition, on which the output of steel in American fixed plants depends. The bargaining table of steel affects all of U.S. labor as a movement. Sensing this, the AFL-CIO also supports the Burke-Hartke concept.

America's Basic Self-Sufficiency

The energy crisis is proving that America is not only a part of the total world but can also plan production well enough to be more self-sufficient than in the past. USWA's bargaining posture in basic steel may help to prove that point.

Where the ownership of basic steel corporations is falling into the hands of conglomerates, it more than likely becomes multinational. However, most of big steel is basically American, investing and producing in its homeland. As such, it could live with Burke-Hartke while stabilizing its production flow and its bargaining table. If this simultaneously serves both workers' and corporate interests, the USWA is never going to accept any criticism that it is not serving America's social and economic needs.

Other Industrial Bargaining

There are many other industrial bargaining styles, too many to develop in any detail here. Volumes have been written about them already.

The details are in membership publications of the respective unions or in theses, dissertations, and other academic work. Each union and its business counterpart, each industry and its bargaining table, are worthy of at least one book. The large and small variations in the bargaining patterns of each industry are more striking when examined in some detail.

The bargaining table in electronics, for instance, is both union shop and open shop. It's open shop with IBM, which has followed the basic and fringe benefit guarantees in the union part of the industry and passed them on with IBM embellishment to its own workers.

It's sometimes open and sometimes union shop with the likes of Honeywell and Sundstrand and Hewlett-Packard. It's usually union shop with Western Electric, Westinghouse, General Electric, RCA.

Electronics: Which Union?

In the electronics industry, the question always is, Which union? The AFL-CIO has a number of affiliated unions that have one or more significant contracts with electronics producers. They include most prominently the construction-related International Brotherhood of Electrical Workers (IBEW) and the International Union of Electrical, Radio and Machine Workers (IUE).

To a considerably lesser extent, the Communications Workers of America (CWA), the American Radio Association, and the Technical Engineers are involved in one or more plants.

A major independent, another "IUE," is also involved in an important way. Once a part of the old CIO, this union lost its affiliation because it was allegedly under some kind of communist influence. The now-independent UE (shorter initials but same full title as the AFL-CIO affiliate that was created to replace it) still does business with major segments of the industry in the northeast. In some cases, it faces the same employers—particularly in the GE/Westinghouse production areas.

General Electric management has for many years been oriented to an industrial relations philosophy of its own making, Boulwarism (simply stated—management knows what is best for the workers, so long as management is relatively benevolent in judging what is best). For many years, GE resisted union group bargaining. If, say, the Machinists, IBEW, IUE (AFL-CIO), and UE (Independent) all had contracts covering a segment of its production force, GE insisted on separate bargaining sessions for separate contracts.

The insistence of a half-dozen unions so situated to bargain a master agreement at the same time and place resulted in legal entanglements, court decisions, strikes, and boycotts before the multiunion bargaining process came into being after the turn of the '60s.

Electronics is not faced with the cohesiveness of the bargaining tables that face steel and auto. Accordingly, conditions of work and agreements are, by comparison, much more diverse. Here, the union bargaining position is not considered to be as strong as in steel and auto—multiunion representation and vast areas of major open shops have contributed to that fact of bargaining life. Additionally, the market has faced the competitive blitz of the Japanese electronic success in consumer items like radios, stereos, and television receivers.

OCAW—New Thrusts to Bargain

The oil and chemical industries still have competing unions and some open shops. The largest and most prominent of the American unions, built from mergers of the old oil workers with one union also in the chemical industry and one in the coke and gas field, is Oil, Chemical and Atomic Workers (OCAW), also an AFL-CIO affiliate.

OCAW has devoted a major share of its recent attention to items that are becoming the hottest priorities on the bargaining table. Oil and chemical refining and distribution are so highly automated that the work force is basically minimal, considering the size of the industry. But wherever the workers are located—whether in Casper or Oklahoma City or Oil City or Beaumont—the problems of the environment and safety are key.

Added to this is the workers' need to have portable pensions. As the wealthier corporations become more automated and more diversified, workers may find themselves in lignite gasification or oil shale retort plants in the future with a different corporate employer. This picture shows why OCAW is beginning the battle for workers' rights and energy say-so in the decades ahead.

To bolster the union's position at the bargaining table with giants like Texaco, Shell, Phillips, American, Gulf, and Conoco, it has added sensitive and knowledgeable staff to its research effort. OCAW has even included a Ph.D. in physics—a woman, "of all things"—to deal with the dangers of pollutants in the workplace and the surrounding communities.

Seeking Public Understanding by Sharing

As OCAW looks to the public and to other trade unions for support, it hasn't kept its research results to itself. Its staffers have written two books—Ray Davidson's *Peril on the Job* (1970) and *Work Is Dangerous to Your Health,* by Jeanne Stellman, Ph.D., and Susan Daum, M.D. (1973).

If OCAW gets its message across to Americans, who are now

acutely reacting to the mid-'70s energy pinch, the producers and suppliers of petrochemical energy might well be forced by the weight of public opinion to agree to pay the several cents per hour that the union proposes for each man-hour of work. With the money so funded, OCAW plans to tackle the environmental dangers surround- ing the production plants.

President Al Grospiron and others in OCAW's leadership know that their union cannot be successful at the bargaining table on this item without public understanding. Although their information cam- paign through books and staff and an informed leadership is at best modest, it is a first in an area that indirectly relates to the life of all Americans.

I would predict their success not only in reaching the excess profits available to the industry, but in needling new kinds of creativity out of the industry's management.

As a mining engineer keenly involved in the technological society and possessing a blend of pragmatism and visionary "propheteering," said, "We can either be a crappy, second-rate society or we can realize a bloom that will embrace us all if petrochemical will invest in its genius and knowledges." And workers are great technicians who dream dreams, too, especially when jobs get dangerous or monotonous.

Another way to put it is that maybe the OCAW emphasis on removing the dangers of the toxic halogens and carbon organisms from workplace, air, and water by a price set on the bargaining table will upgrade the effort on the employers' side of that table.

The citizen cannot fail to profit—even to making safer the chem- ical composition of insecticides that are sprayed on his food during growing seasons. The industrial bargaining table has great potential; it has a multitude of positive side effects for all people.

MANY OTHER INDUSTRIAL AREAS

The bargaining table problems in the many other areas of major production in the nation can be dealt with only in passing, just to point out the multitude of factors involved.

For instance, the merger of the A.F. of L. and CIO did not require the merger of unions that often faced each other in competi- tive jurisdictions. This has been a factor in what kind of contracts are bargained with which employer.

In paper and wood pulp production, it took 16 years for the two major unions (Papermakers and Paperworkers; Pulp, Sulphite and Paper Mill Workers), each with memberships over 150,000, to unite as one union, the United Paperworkers. Bargaining patterns may change where competition between unions is thus eliminated. In due time, we can judge the effects on both sides of the paper/pulp table—workers and employers.

Rubber—Much Local Emphasis

The United Rubber, Cork, and Plastic Workers of America (URW) has the field to itself in rubber, but not necessarily in plastics.

URW bargains with big rubber (Goodyear, Firestone, Goodrich, U.S.) on separate bases, as does UAW in auto. But the union also faces smaller producers in the tire business and many producers in various facets of the rubber and plastics markets—for instance, Gates Rubber, the world's largest fan belt manufacturer. As a result, URW tries to set policy guidelines in national conferences of representative locals. However, the local unions at the headquarters plant areas set the pace with each of the firms. A pattern is usually a strong guideline, but local unions have different contract conditions depending upon the plant they represent.

To compare rubber with auto and steel is to say that these unions each set their own independent patterns, yet they look to each other for both guidelines and results. For example, there is a Ford contract across all Ford plants and there are local plant "supplementary" contracts. The same is true for GM and Chrysler. Steel has a basic master agreement across 90 percent of the industry; the local unions also bargain supplementary agreements for in-plant administration, job assignment, apprenticeship programs, and grievance procedures. Rubber generally has local union-local plant agreements, but that is not to say there are not similarities between plants, employers, and even industries. In 1975 OCAW and URW agreed that they had enough in common to bring the question of merging the unions to a vote.

Meat-Packing: A Major Shift

Another major industrial area is meat-packing. The major geographical and modernization shift in the '50s and '60s in that industry had a drastic effect on the bargaining unions—the former CIO Packinghouse Workers and the broader-jurisdiction A.F. of L. Amalgamated Meat Cutters and Butcher Workmen of North America (AMCBW).

Stockyards have moved from the big cities or have decreased in size. Some Midwest city majors (Swift, Morell, Wilson, Armour, Cudahy) have kept only packaging operations in the cities or have automated their plants, causing massive layoffs. The huge feedlot operations across the Midwest and the High Plains states have spawned smaller, modernized packing plants in nearby towns or adjacent acreages. The production lines have turned out more processed meats with fewer people in a decentralized setting.

In some cases, of course, smaller cities like the Siouxs (Falls and City) have been able to adapt to the decentralization because they have not been as choked up as the industrial big cities.

The Packinghouse Workers had their membership in the big cities. The AMCBW had both the apprenticeable craft of the retail and wholesale meatcutters plus many of the smaller packers—and here and there a plant of the major packers. AMCBW did not suffer severe membership losses by the movers and the modernizers; Packinghouse did. So they merged in the '60s under the AMCBW label. Better than a half million strong, they have kept the countryside pretty well organized.

The union and the industry are interesting.

Major packers are not necessarily the pace-setters at the bargaining tables. Mushrooming packers like Iowa Beef and Monfort of Colorado became large in small cities. The two companies present a study in contrasts. Iowa built company fences to keep the union out at Dakota City, Iowa; it failed. Monfort weathered a strike but has both bargained a contract favorable to both sides of the table and employed extensively from the minority side of the tracks—the seasonal farm laborers. They are mainly Chicano, who have become year-round taxpaying citizens instead of winter welfare recipients.

This transformation of an otherwise affluent agricultural countryside and small city has extended a new spirit among many slum neighborhoods of rural America. The union has been a cooperative factor in expanding the work force into the disadvantaged neighborhoods of farmland America. They have signed agreements with Monfort and others in Heartland USA to prove their good faith and mutual responsibilities with management.

Poultry: New Production and Union Members

Among the new automated agribusiness establishments is the special plant industry of poultry processing. Here, AMCBW has moved with progressive strides, too. The new union units in poultry reflect the new equality demands put upon the American employer—as many as or more women than men; the minority communities heavily involved (black in states like Texas and Arkansas, Chicano in the West and Southwest).

Put all of this bargaining table expansion together as AMCBW has been able to do, and note where the memberships are and what their ethnic and national backgrounds represent. You can conclude with me why this union understood the Midwestern liberalism of Senator McGovern and was one of the first to stand on his behalf. This action was in marked contrast to the political reticence of some unions in the heavy industrial centers, where Wallace and Nixon made marked inroads on both leadership and membership.

Otherwise, the bargaining tables of AMCBW and UAW and USWA have more in common among their respective members, even though, by comparison, AMCBW has a multitude of fixed plant agreements. AMCBW also has within its ranks a large craft segment, now greatly enlarged by the supermarket retailing policies of packaged meats. The meatcutters of the past are still needed but not in the same numbers, out front, facing the customer; here, again, the meat-wrappers include a majority of women. AMCBW is more than an industrial union, yet it has extended the industrial union benefit to rural America as no other union has.

The Other Basics: Construction and Transportation

When it comes to defining where bargaining power means the most in the American economy, the commercial construction and basic transportation industries rank in importance with basic industry.

The skilled construction crafts have been in evidence for the entire century, as have the railroad unions. The latter are heavily "fraternal" and call themselves brotherhoods.

In transportation, a larger proportion of the total operating work force is organized. In this sense, it matches the younger but vigorous industrial unions. It may be surprising to note that the least well organized are the building trades.

Where the major builders are at work—in heavy commercial construction, in most federally funded projects like reclamation and highways, and in apartment and condominium construction—the skilled crafts are well organized. Where the membership is not so evident is in small commercial construction, many prefabricated types of buildings, and individual and small-development home construction—yet the latter area provides employment for almost half of the construction industry's workers.

In both transportation and construction, the unions face innumerable employers at an almost innumerable number of bargaining tables through more than 50 different national and international unions. This multiplicity of business firms and of unions creates a variety of bargaining styles, ranging from effective to ineffective on both sides of the table. In a marked contrast with heavy-industry bargaining processes, there is a less predictable pattern because there are so many examples on which to generalize.

TRANSPORTATION

Who Does the Busing?

Bus transport depends upon the employer almost more than the union that deals with the employer.

If the employer is public, the employee is probably not under union agreement. It is even possible that the right of the bus drivers to strike is considered illegal by statute or executive proclamation. School bus drivers are not likely either to receive recognition or to have signed union agreements with boards of education or school committees.

Local transit systems carrying passengers for fares are more likely to be organized, whether publicly or privately owned, and operate under signed agreements, even if the union cannot strike a public employer.

Long-haul bus systems have the most sophisticated of the bargained agreements. They have been organized over a period of many decades and have neither relinquished nor legally been ordered to cease the use of the strike.

And Who Does the Trucking?

The energy crisis of early 1974 brought truckers in America to the public's attention. Don't confuse most of those truckers, however, with either the Teamsters or the over-the-road major truck lines that carry the daily freight of the land. They were the so-called independents, who were affected by the crisis in the oil industry perhaps more than anyone else. With the nation not knowing quite which way either its own national leadership or the world was going, the independent truckers took the stance of militant response. Although what they did was not necessarily pleasant, it was not unlike many other explosive reactions of groups of people in American history.

Because the independent truckers did not have the experience or the sophistication of the long-haul major carriers and the Teamsters, they conducted a "strike" of their own—against both the government and the oil industry. Normally, strikes come at the end of a bargaining process where the two parties fail to agree. Such was not the case with the independents.

Because they had no bargaining process, they used guns—fortunately, only in a few instances—and put up picket lines and roadblocks. They aimed to stop the truckers—Teamsters—who had the bargaining process. It was a strange kind of a strike, led by frustrated people who, in anger and disillusionment, had nowhere else to turn.

The difference between these two segments of American truckers is simple—economics.

About 50 percent of the big-rig drivers in America were independents. The other half worked for major interstate truck carriers that operate scheduled runs carrying all kinds of freight. The latter belonged to the Teamsters union.

The independents were caught in two binds. One was the major increase in diesel and other fuel products. They hadn't bid for jobs or hauls with this in mind. Not operating in large fleets, they found that they had to keep their trucks on the road longer hours; they were generally unable to recoup business losses in freight tonnage because they had less ton-mile capacity. Then 70-mph speed limits were cut to 55-mph. If they had been scheduling five trips a week, it became four; their load capacities were reduced up to 20 percent.

Didn't the long-haul, scheduled lines suffer the same way? Yes, but when you provide scheduled freight service, you run whether full or not; you figure light loads along with full loads in your cost estimating. When the energy crunch came, they had the advantage of scheduling fewer trips and fuller loads.

What about the Teamsters? Their contracts often provided both hourly (time) and mileage factors. If the slower speeds meant fewer miles driven, the hourly guarantees for the longer hours picked up slack. Their employers were hurting more than they. The union was able to lend a hand here. They had the one big-union president in America who had been consistent in his politics, as unrepresentative as that consistency was to the views of most union members. Frank Fitzsimmons was on the White House team; he could talk for both his members and their employers.

The independents include thousands of truckers who own their own tractors and haul anyone's trailer or rig. There are also thousands of others who do specialized hauling exclusively for a particular business or contractor. The independent trucker may even be purchasing or leasing his tractor from the same business or contractor for whom he hauls. Like the newsboy who carries the paper to the home, this trucker is an independent businessman.

More than likely, he belongs to a trade association, but not for the sake of bargaining with an employer. He belongs for a variety of other reasons, only a few of which relate to the economics of his business. As an independent businessman, the lower his mileage costs, the better off he considers himself to be. Accordingly, he has had his independent opportunity to drive faster and longer hours in order to "cash in on the buck"; he has not worked for an employer who figures out his drivers' benefits along with his other costs as part of an agreement that puts reasonable safety limitations upon the hours of driving and very satisfactory benefits into the pocketbook of the worker. And workers do not normally share any responsibility directly with the employer for his return on capital investment and operating profit.

If the difference between the independent and the Teamster driver had not been apparent before, it became apparent in 1974.

The long-haul truck lines provide the strong base of the Teamsters union. They also provide the strongest base in the automotive mechanic and repair field for the Machinists. The bargaining tables are separate. The contracts, however, are more than likely handled by a multiemployer bargaining combine. In trucking, however, the combine is not usually the multi-industry and multibusiness grouping discussed in the first part of this chapter; it is only a trucking employer combine.

Bus, subway, and commuter rail transportation in urban areas is generally related to the Amalgamated Transit Union (ATU), although New York and other northeastern states have substantial Transport Workers Union of America (TWU) areas. Urban transport is usually handled by only one public or private utility in an area. The two AFL-CIO unions are not necessarily side-by-side competitors, therefore.

As noted earlier, TWU also has airline contracts; ATU has the major interstate bus lines in most of the nation. Both, however, utilize the industrial concept of organization—the mechanics, maintenance, and even office forces (in some areas) are part of the operators' unions.

Teamsters: Organized to be Effective

The Teamsters inevitably come up with *standard* rate and working-conditions provisions in their long-haul drivers' and warehousemen's contracts—not just because of the multiunit employer bargaining combine they face but because they have adjusted their bargaining to major geographical bargaining areas that they try to balance off. They call these areas conferences. The conference (such as the Western Conference of Teamsters) also provides a structural way to deal with with state, within-state, and more-than-one-state councils. The chief officers of the councils meet regularly; the same officers meet periodically in their respective conferences.

The council-conference organizational structure gives the Teamsters great strength at the bargaining tables. Since the great bulk of the membership is scattered through thousands of bargaining units, they need to have strong bonds of unity.

The warehouse and miscellaneous group of employers in larger cities face a particular local union at the bargaining table. Sometimes two local unions overlap in these jurisdictions, but the second local will deal primarily with delivery drivers—of all kinds except probably milk drivers and bakery wagon drivers, which may have separate locals.

Additionally, the over-the-road drivers' locals, with regional or national contracts, will service other jurisdictions of the Teamsters organization—airline employees, office workers (not organized in connection with other Teamsters operations), automotive mechanics (where not IAM in large truck shops), race track employees, etc.

The truck lines usually have a separate warehousemen's local; the noncommon carrier warehouses (like those in the supermarkets, wholesale distributors) have separate locals; the construction drivers, who primarily relate to the AFL-CIO building trades unions, are separate; the chauffeurs and taxi drivers may have separate local unions, too.

Exceptions to these general conditions of local unions are the single-purpose locals that sometimes are located in middle-sized cities. These are usually catchalls for the specialized areas where the big cities have separate locals—delivery drivers, milk drivers, local warehousemen, and so on. Often, the line drivers, construction drivers, and trucking dock workers and warehousemen are in locals that cover an area of a state, of parts of several states, or a total state.

Most Contracts Locally Bargained

To get to the bargaining table aspect of this union, which is the largest in America, most locals bargain with their own employers at local levels. That is why the council and conference policies are so important to the local business manager and agents. On the other hand, the multiemployer over-the-road truck lines and the mail order house contracts (mainly Montgomery Ward) are not ordinarily locally bargained, though they are locally administered. Sometimes, however, retail outlets of mail order department stores are locally bargained.

If there is a mixed bag within one American union, it is in the independent Teamsters.

Their relationship to the produce growers, especially in California and Arizona, was noted earlier. They also compete with many smaller AFL-CIO jurisdictions, especially in the office areas where the Office and Professional Employees (OPEIU), AFL-CIO, still operates from a point of organizational weakness. The long-standing policy of local Teamster support of OPEIU in truck line offices has more recently become one of either a blurred or a directly competitive organizational policy.

Teamsters, then, are interested in more than long-haul trucking—but it is the long-haul driver who is at the top of the scale and the center of Teamsters' attention. And the bargaining table possesses unusual strength in this area, since long-haul trucks move much of America's freight. When the bargaining reaches an impasse, there is always the threat of shutdown. Such a strike could affect one or more of the major regions of America or it could be nationwide.

Rail Unions under Stress

When it comes to rail unions, the Teamsters stand with the trucking industry first. Whether out-of-date management set back rail lines since the late '20s or if it was the simple advent of automotive trucks and vehicles that dealt the major blow, the railroad industry and railroad unions have not found the legislative climate in the 50 states favorable; often the trucking and highway lobbies, aided to some extent by the Teamsters, have been major adversaries of the railroads.

The bargaining table of the rail industry has been a multiunion operation until recently, when most of the operating brotherhoods merged into the United Transportation Union (UTU). The separate crafts of conductors, brakemen, porter-brakemen, firemen, oilers, and enginemen (about half of the nation's engineers) have become a united industrial type union to operate the long-haul and intercity rail lines.

In the meantime, the more aggressive long-haul rail freight lines west of Chicago have been merging or trying to merge, or have survived as separate entities because of good freight base rates and highly automated freight yards and main-line trackage. They have also shut down branch and feeder lines wherever they could get away with it.

It is difficult to say whether or not the passenger traffic in the more congested Northeast is primarily responsible for the economic demise of former giants like the Penn Central and the Erie Lackawanna. Nevertheless, it has made bargaining somewhat different for the operating and nonoperating (Boilermakers, Machinists, Electrical Workers, Sheet Metal Workers, Carmen, etc.) brotherhoods in the East than the same unions with the more profitable systems of the West. There are the farm-belt systems, many of which protrude well into the West or South, too, that do not necessarily paint themselves as patrons of prosperity like the L & N, Monon, Illinois Central, Missouri Pacific—just to name a few. And it is likewise with the Eastern lines that head for the Midwest or South—like Seaboard, Atlantic Coast, C&O.

Shifting the Burden

Management has tried for many years to put the burden on the backs of the rail unions—especially the operating unions—for the rail industry's inability to compete in the passenger traffic world, let alone the freight hauls.

The rail unions didn't sign agreements in their early days; they operated on work rules written into company policy books; they didn't think in terms of union shops, but few operating employees did not belong to their respective brotherhoods.

Now UTU combines the crafts for operations; signs union shop agreements with the major rail systems; and has fought to make certain firemen were not laid off as the diesel replaced the steam-driven trains. If this "featherbedding," as the rail operators call it for public consumption, caused nonprofitable rail operation, then the multiplicity of executive positions that simultaneously continued to exist in the rail industry at much higher salaries should have been on the bargaining table, also.

Who and how many serve in management has not been a bargainable issue in labor-management relations, however. Who and how many serve in the work force represented by the union unit is always on the bargaining table by implication—even though management retains the right to determine who is employed. This implication in rail and all American industry is wrapped up in bargained policies for apprenticeship, job classifications, layoff provisions, rehire requirements, and other areas. But not for management!

So featherbedding in the nonmanagement rail work force has become the talk of the public; featherbedding in the executive work force is seldom in public conversation. Rail unions either failed in their efforts or never really pressed the point of "who is featherbedding whom."

Rail unions have always faced governmental regulation. In times of war and emergency, they have been government operated. The Railroad Retirement Act was a precursor of many public employee retirement systems as well as of the Social Security system.

Like governmental retirement systems (federal and many state and some local governmental), the Railroad Retirement Act removed the major provisions of retirement security from the bargaining table. It further separated railroad retirement from Social Security rather than as a supplementary plan. Lastly, it locks in a shrinking work force to the system of employment and literally condemns the railroad employee to stick it out.

Portability—Bargaining Unlocks Issue

This whole concept may be changed even in rail bargaining if Congress acts upon legislation in the mid-'70s to establish full portability of pension plans from one employer to another. Bargainers in other industries have used the Social Security system as a base for their health and welfare retirement benefits. The legislation passed by Congress in 1974 was a first small step toward portability.

The adaptation to the Social Security base provides a minimum amount of portability—namely, a worker carries his Social Security benefits with him unless he moves to employment in the railroads, the federal government, or many state and local governments.

The Railroad Retirement Act does limit the bargaining table for rail employees.

At the time of the First World War, of course, rails were as essential as water transportation. The rubber-tired vehicles weren't yet in the mainstream, and the airways were focusing on the single-seat fighter and the new bombers. Rails were in their economic heyday, and changes were not yet apparent. In the Second World War, there was a fear that the supplies of natural rubber would be cut off, and so military vehicles would have to get whatever rubber there was. Thus, the more mobile and adaptable trucks and buses would have to give way to rail transport.

Polyester cord was rushed in quantity from the great synthetic plants of America; rails moved much freight, true, and most long-haul domestic troop contingents; but the Depression and the highly competitive truck industry had taken such a toll of the rail industry that it was not able to regain the advantage that it held afer the First War.

Congress and the state legislatures have catered more to the truckers than the railroaders. The teamsters have grown stronger at the bargaining table because the truck lines have grown in size and significance, and the rail unions have found the going as tough in the legislative halls as they have at the bargaining tables.

Compulsory Arbitration—Handle with Care

Congress has even gone so far as to slap a one-time compulsory-arbitration law on the rail unions. It said in effect, the public doesn't like your work rules. Of course, it didn't look at the work rules of rail management. It didn't look severely at the work rules of the American military, either. It was collectively soothed by not being required to look at the other work rules in society, including its own.

In Congress, both conservatives and liberals joined against the compulsory arbitration moves, though for basically different reasons. The honest conservative (there never have been many in Congress if the voting records can be used for proof) does not like to interfere with any part of the bargaining table—he counts on management to look after private management, not the legislator. The honest liberal (voting records also note them as not being numerous) also believes in the freedom to bargain, but primarily as a worker's need.

But most congressmen react to slogans and to the members of the public who speak out. Featherbedding and work rules were in their minds, bargaining tables notwithstanding. Fortunately, the two concepts were applied to only one industry—railroading.

In the late '60s, to avoid a rail strike, Congress opted for compulsory arbitration in the one instance. The result: two-man crews in the cab of a diesel locomotive would be phased out. Subsequently, rail crossing accidents have more than doubled across the nation, but the arbitration rule stands.

The detail of the settlement outside the scope of the bargaining table is not so important as the issue of compulsory arbitration or some modification of it. It is discussed here as an aside to rail unions in competition with any other kind of transportation unions.

The bargaining teams of all unions (except for a limited number of public employee unions that feel they must accept third-party settlement of a dispute) reject compulsory arbitration as a settlement of an impasse in contract negotiations.

Arbitration: Sometimes "Yes"

Please note that the rejection is qualified: ". . . impasse in contract negotiations." Many unions have strong contract provisions for using some form of arbitration—usually a binding or compulsory form—as the last step in the settlement of a grievance between a worker and management.

American unions are not ready to have the bargaining tables controlled by either labor courts (as in Australia) or third-party binding arbitration. The strike, which is in fact used in a very minimal way in terms of worker-days lost in American industry, is still the last step in the bargaining process to the union bargaining teams.

If oil is in short supply for a limited number of years or even in the long run, perhaps in a few decades the Teamsters will be looking at a declining truck industry as the UTU faces a sick railroad business. Perhaps, too, the Amtrak national passenger train systems will bring newer and more exciting train travel back to both commuters and intercity travelers in the nation.

If so, both bus and truck transportation will find rail lines more competitive. Rail unions will respond by updating their bargaining agendas.

Air Transport—Energy, Petro, and Unions

In air transport, jet power depends on petroleum, though it could depend upon alternate sources in the future. Crude oil is not in short supply in America; industry simply has not developed it. Their reason is that it is not yet economic.

The price of gasification plants in the trillion-barrel central and northern Plains and Mountain states, developed reasonably within environmentally acceptable patterns, is within reach of profitable private venture. Likewise, liquid supplies of petroleum in the same area could exceed the known worldwide supplies of over 400 billion barrels. The book cliffs of the Green River and Colorado River upper basin (Wyoming, Colorado, and Utah) have more petroleum for retort out of oil shale mines than the estimators can estimate (over a trillion barrels in immediate sight).

Thus, while airline travel was disturbed superficially by the immediate energy crisis of the 1970s, it will become more profitable because of larger ships carrying larger cargo and passenger loads with fewer flights and no major additions to crews and maintenance personnel. If air travel were faced with a single union jurisdiction, like long-haul trucking, the bargaining table would significantly change. As it is, multiple jurisdictions maintain variable conditions between and among air carriers and within classifications of employees.

Not all of the cockpit crews in the big ten of the Amercan airways belong to the Air Line Pilots Association—independent and Teamsters unions cut into the bargaining pattern—but ALPA dominates the craft jobs up front on airlines that fly the globe. But when ALPA strikes, only two or three carriers are outside its scope. If conditions are good and "pilots live like kings," as many say, it is only because they have the most sensitive jobs in the industry, and no traveler or airlines employee disputes the assertion in public.

ALPA—A Contract for Safety

Pilots have helped via the union contract to do more than financially enrich both their flying days and their early-retirement plan. They have given the traveler the confidence that statistics prove out: just about the safest way to get there is to fly commercially. Where ALPA contracts are in force, safety is paramount, even to the point of practicing all cockpit operations, including takeoff and touchdown, after layoffs or lengthy vacation periods.

The captain, the first officer, the second officer, and the flight engineer (navigator) know what that contract means and rigidly enforce it, just as they expect airline management to exercise the responsibilities of enforcement.

By using the bargaining technique, the cockpit crew has become the elite of American labor. In terms of the movement, they affiliate as ALPA, even though they almost do not belong, politically or economically, to the working class. Nevertheless, if the Airline Machinists (mechanics and maintenance crews) put up their pickets on the aprons of the airports, the cockpit crew doesn't march right by. ALPA pickets, too, but it doesn't need to. When ALPA members don't show for work, nothing flies. A plane at rest in the hangar or on the runway doesn't demand to be cleaned out, serviced with food and beverage, mechanically checked, refueled, or served by stewards or stewardesses. No one works.

Multiple contracts and jurisdictions are still not without union recognition and benefit. It's just the fact that there is little comparing of notes with each other—including those in the ticket offices, programming the computers, manning the airport counters, and handling the baggage and air freight. The lower echelons suffer; but most of them bargain.

BUILDING TRADES AND THEIR CRAFTS

The miracle of a Sears or Hancock Tower in Chicago; Empire State or World Trade Center top hats in New York; the overpowering antenna higher than any building near Fargo's Red River North; the Hoover, Glen Canyon, Grand Coulee, Muscle Shoals, or St. Lawrence waterway giants; the Verrazano Narrows or Golden Gate bridges; Pennsylvania's pioneer turnpike, New York's Lincoln or Holland tunnels; or Straight Creek's Eisenhower or Moffat's railroad shortcut tunneling of the crest of the Continent—in all these and other engineering and architectural marvels of America, there were men and machines involved.

The man who has been there, hard hat and tools, knows.

Engineers and architects dreamed and created, and a man-made bloom was put on the face of America. The venture capital and risk of life and limb came from the contractors and the laborers and the craftsmen of the construction industry.

When building and rebuilding ceases in America, the nation will cease.

The building needs in America are greater than ever. Construction genius of the craftsmen on the job can contribute in increasing proportions to the stability of economic growth, the safety and usability of the completed project, and the ecological health of the communities around the products of the building trades.

Share Little Praise

Yet the building trades unions in America gain little praise for their contribution to the material blessings of our lives and shoulder more than their share of the blame for what seems to be wrong with America in the 1970s.

Who are the building trades?

Within the movement—within the AFL-CIO—they are all the construction crafts except the truck driver, who is a Teamster. They include the elitists of the blue-collar workers—IBEW (electricians) and United Association (plumbers and fitters). I jokingly refer to them in conversation as being to the building trades what the MDs are to the professions. It is unfair to say they are the most skilled. This is one of the problems in the craft union structure—what other skilled trades compare themselves to as they look at the "mainline" crafts.

To continue, there are the Operating Engineers, Bridge, Structural, and Ornamental Iron Workers, Elevator Constructors, Asbestos

Workers (and Heat and Frost Insulators), Boilermakers (Iron Ship Builders, Blacksmiths, Forgers), Bricklayers (and Masons and Plasterers); Lathers (Wood, Wire and Metal) and as the on-site backup for the Plasterers, Painters and Allied Trades (Carpet and Linoleum Layers, Glassworkers and Glaziers, Bill Posters and Sign Painters), Plasterers and Cement Masons, Roofers (Damp and Waterproof Workers—United Slate, Tile and Composition), Sheet Metal Workers, and Tile and Marble Setters.

The Basic Crafts; the Largest Unions

Pointedly omitted to this point are the basic craft and helpers—the two largest union jurisdictions in the construction trades. They are the Carpenters and Joiners (which includes the Millwrights and perhaps soon the Lathers) and the Laborers International Union of North America.

Actually, the largest union in the building trades is the IBEW—one of the few American unions, along with the Carpenters, to top 800,000 members—but it has local unions in the electrical shops, in the production of electrical equipment, in both construction and maintenance of utilities, and in industrial electronics (such as Western Electric manufacturing). Their members in these areas outnumber the apprenticeable journeyman construction craft electricians. With the carpenters, they have members in some of the new prefab industrial plants and cabinetmaking shops, but their basic membership is in the on-site construction field.

The laborers are branching out into some public-sector jurisdictions and also prefabricating plants, especially prestressed concrete. Basically, though, the laborer is the "skilled helper" to the basic crafts—especially in site clearance, site clean-up, heavy-equipment operation, and the trowel trade (brick and cement masons, in particular).

Building Trades Department and Councils

How do these various crafts bargain?

Within the House of Labor, they have a department that is central to the strength of the former A.F. of L. in the AFL-CIO. The department charters councils.

Building trades councils seek to have the above-mentioned crafts support and cooperate with each other. The councils support themselves by council cards purchased by number, not by name, by the local unions. The purchase number does not necessarily coincide with the real membership of the local union.

There are two basic reasons for this.

One is just plain dishonesty—the union either doesn't expect the council to do much on behalf of its members or else the union officers find other excuses built around their local budgets to "economize." The other reason is more likely. The local union represents more than construction workers—this is particularly true of the Electricians, Sheet Metal Workers, and Plumbers and Fitters, who represent manufacturing, sales, and maintenance shops and businesses as well.

Do the building trades councils bargain?

Yes, they do, indirectly if not directly.

In the bargained relationship that exists between the heavy or general contractors (most of which are organized through AGC— Associated General Contractors—across the country) and certain of the building crafts, the councils are usually parties to those contracts in the geographical areas where the councils operate.

Since some general contractors—in fact, the prominent ones— operate across state lines, different conditions may exist from one council jurisdiction to another. Sometimes, different conditions exist between the local general contractors and the out-of-state general contractor who moves a work force into a local area.

One thing is certain: The conditions on union construction jobs are never lower than the wages, fringes, and work rules set down in the general contract of the council in the area.

The Basic "General" Contract

The basic contract with the general contractor will usually contain at least two of the crafts, generally Laborers and Carpenters. Both unions have permanent cadre members on daily hire with the large general operators.

General contractors hire out of the union hiring halls, too, which have been modified to conform to National Labor Relations Board (NLRB) rules. NLRB operates under Taft-Hartley, which outlaws the closed shop. An exclusive hiring hall is a closed shop—in other words, the employer calls the union to employ (for one day or one year or for life) a worker.

If the closed shop were legal, the building trades would opt for it. For all practical purposes, both general contractors and American maritime industrialists still rely heavily on labor supplied through union hiring halls—thus, the NLRB has tended to be flexible on the waterfront and in construction.

However, the employer can hire anyone he wishes from any source. In construction, most unions and union contractors have agreed that if the person first employed outside the union hiring hall is retained more than seven days by the contractor, that person's name goes on the hiring hall board of the union. In simpler terms, if the person hired directly by the contractor is laid off, he is in the union's jurisdiction and entitled to the protection of the union agreement with the same or any other related contractor. He also joins the union.

This special condition has its problems on both sides of the street. It is hard to apply to the apprenticeable trades—the skilled mechanical and trowel crafts. Here, historical conditions, as modified by equal-employment-opportunity laws in some states and now by the federal government, provide for apprenticeable periods averaging three to four years, after which the apprentice becomes a journeyman.

Without debating the merits of apprenticeship here—in my opinion, subject to reasonable modification in any field of work including those now using the process, it is basic to job know-how and should be used universally—the journeyman is the person the employer really wants on a job. One week of work, even in a helping capacity in the construction crafts, does little to qualify a person for work on either short-term or long-term construction projects. Primarily, this rule helps contractors who find mechanically skilled persons in the non-union work force who have not gone through registered apprenticeship (which is jointly administered by contractors and union leaders). It also is readily applicable to construction laborers, where big contractors want to exercise their own hiring advantage (favors to college-bound youth, friends, or even to reach into the ethnic minority communities to meet "quotas" under local building plans).

So, the general contractors who want a union work force sign contracts with certain general crafts and the building trades councils. The contract inevitably includes the provision that all building trades must require—all special skills and crafts not covered by the general contract must go to a "fair" subcontract shop (that is, a union shop).

Subcontracting—Part of the Craft Structure

The construction crafts that are usually involved with specialty or subcontractor shops include practically everyone, from electricians to bricklayers.

Operating engineers—who operate the heavy equipment, do site preparation, hoist equipment by cranes to the high-rise workplace, do the earth moving and the pavement laying—are, like the carpenter, generally part of the general contractor's work force.

The subcontract crafts bargain their own agreements, each with their own shops. Across the geographical area of a building trades council, they deal with multiemployer bargaining—in other words, all shops have the same conditions in the same area. Again, when their respective employers do business outside the area of the building trades council where the business is established, the minimum conditions of the area in which the work is performed must be met.

Subcontracts usually also define where the contractor is to obtain his work force (within the legal limits of NLRA, of course). It often happens that a traveling-card journeyman is either brought in from an area of oversupply of the same craft to do a local job or a local journeyman may be among those the contractor takes into the other jurisdiction to do his work.

Checking out the Nonunion Jobs

Building trades councils are more than just parties to contracts with general contractors, crafts, and helpers. They also check jobs—especially ones that are nonunion.

If the job has federal or state money in any part, they try to determine if the nonunion general and subcontractors are meeting prevailing standards. It used to be prevailing wages—at the federal level, the Davis-Bacon Fair Labor Standards Act and amendments now include fringes benefits in that determination. The union contractor must set aside an amount of money per man per hour for retirement, health, and vacation payments and trusts. In many instances, this adds up to 20 percent of the base rate of pay.

If the building trades council agent suspects that the contractors are not meeting the requirements of law, he tries to ascertain the facts. This is not easy to do—even when states have prevailing wages or standards orders. Procedures are set forth; the contractors usually file their rate and fringe benefits for various crafts on the jobs, but the individual's actual paycheck is private.

The nonunion operator can evade the law and the eagle eye of the building trades in several ways.

First, he might have someone work eight hours and credit the worker shorter hours—say, seven. Why doesn't the worker report this? Seven times the union hourly scale may be more than he's ever seen before, and so he agrees to secrecy before he's hired.

Second, the contractor might say that the fringes begin after the third or sixth month of employment. This is the pattern of many retirement benefits: wait awhile before funding! If the job is finished in less than the months required for qualifying, the worker carries no fringe benefits with him to the next contractor ("You have Social Security and workmen's compensation and unemployment insurance," is the mouthful the worker hears as he comes on board or when he exits for the next workplace).

Most workers, including union craftsmen, understand little about the operation of law—even more than that, they sometimes believe that laws are more all-inclusive than they are. So, a contractor-employer on a nonunion construction site can get away with this second saving. (Even union apprentice schooling is highly deficient in terms of putting economics, labor law, citizenship understanding, or analysis of trade union structure into the training.)

Third, and even more prevalent, the nonunion contractor can underclassify the worker—unless he is a basic laborer, in which case it is difficult to pay less per hour than the lowest scale of pay filed with the appropriate federal or state agency (if the requirement prevails, that is—in some states, it does not). For instance, the employer might put a person on as a truck driver without a helper and classify him as a truck driver-helper, explaining to the worker that all this means is that he helps to load and unload as well as drive the truck. Needless to say, a truck driver-helper gets a lower rate of pay.

He might have the worker do a sheet metal or fitters rate job but tell him that this is the carpenter's jurisdiction on his job, carrying a slighter lower rate. Or, cement finishing is a laborer's job, the foreman says—and so on.

Getting at the Facts to Correct the Situation

The building trades agent might track down a worker who admits that he is underclassified; he might convince the worker that he is being treated worse than the law provides; and he might find the worker laid off before he can pursue the matter. The worker, then, feeling that he cannot file a claim through a federal or state agency without being blacklisted or that the legal representation will cost too much, does not give consent for the union representative to follow through.

Going the other route, the building trades agent seeks out the governmental agency involved in the contracting or in the funding of the contractor. But if that agency does not move to get a fair union contractor on the job, his effort could fail. At least the agent might pinpoint a government employee on whom an elected official might bring some pressure to enforce the law. Otherwise, he can help the various crafts trying to organize the work force on the nonunion site. He has the weapon of showing the workers that they are being cheated by their employer(s) under the law. Even here, the building trades "rep" may find that some of the crafts he is trying to aid are reluctant to take nonjourneymen mechanics into their own union hall.

The point in this latter case is clear—no union wants to cut the standards of its own training program and craft; the admission of anyone with less training and/or craft skill gives the contractor the talking point at the next negotiations of creating new job classifications at lower or in-between rates of pay. If agreed to, he could then assign the lower-classified worker to work previously performed by the journeyman mechanic.

All of these factors are relative, of course, particularly if the journeyman at $10 per hour turns out both quality and quantity well above an $8 rated worker. Conversely, some contractors in construction trades argue for good or ill that any young worker at any rate is potentially better than any older worker—the exceptions balancing out. (So go the arguments, at least.)

A Strong Bargaining Table

The bargaining table has been strong in the building crafts, particularly since the Wagner Act. Contractors and union representatives have found much in common through the system of training the skilled mechanic on the job and in the classroom. Like lawyers, architects, doctors, dentists, and engineers, the journeyman craftsman stands better than a nine out of ten chance of retiring from or dying on the job. The lack of turnover is important to the success of the union contractor. It is the one economic advantage he has over the large nonunion employer, who still has to search out from the general market whomever he can find to fill his bill of particulars.

The union contractor can look to a higher degree of labor cost efficiency, accordingly. Only the small nonunion contractor who does not seek major contracts can build efficiency into his own permanent work cadre (the larger the contractor's operation becomes, the smaller the proportion of permanent workers on his payroll). A permanent work cadre, union or nonunion, becomes a faithful and loyal employee group—but even in the nonunion instance, the good employee remains only because he is well compensated for his skill and faithful support of his employer.

Since the advent of the signed agreement as the standard practice in union construction, the provisions cover more than simple job classification and scale rates. Seasonal layoffs because of weather, climate, or private capital requirements have been softened by health-welfare-pension trust provisions and an hourly reserve to use annually in the same way that the 52-week employee gets paid vacation time.

In the days before the written agreement, the hourly rate in the building trades had to include the personally disciplined savings habits of the worker and his family. In the North and West, where wintery blasts or long rainy seasons interfere with the construction workdays, it used to be that any laborer or craftsman was fortunate to obtain at least nine months of work each year.

Internal Disputes

The building crafts are not without their internal troubles. Where their respective leaders can maintain effective discipline among themselves, they have a way of persuading the union subcontracted craft to stay off an otherwise nonunion job.

Let me describe this more specifically, though cautioning that "Any material that follows is fictional, and any reference that seems to portray real people or events or union situations is without fact and is strictly coincidental."

A nonunion general contractor gets a major job. He lines up totally nonunion subcontractors. He hires laborers off the street, but he needs skilled carpenters and operating engineers for site clearance, for setting forms for footings and foundations, and for general carpentry and heavy-equipment operation throughout the project. Union engineers and union carpenters are the only ones that he can get.

The union craftsmen hire on the job. The building trades council gets complaints from the mechanical crafts, who work for union subs, generally. The council votes to place an informational picket on the general contractor's work site. The engineers and the carpenters go to work, anyway. They literally say to the other crafts, Go out and organize your craft at that work site. The sparks fly. Building trades agents quit.

Another example is that of a large nonunion home builder who finds that he needs union plumbers on all his construction jobs and that the electrical codes are so well standardized that he needs a master electrician on cadre and an electrician journeyman on each work site at the appropriate time. The plumbers and electricians are union members. They go to work side by side with the nonunion carpenters, laborers, roofers, glaziers, and others. The crafts that are being discriminated against stand up in the building trades council and contend that the "entire job would be union except for you guys who scab on us by working side by side with the other scabs."

With the separation of unions and the large nonunion home building industry, aided by right-to-work laws and Taft-Hartley's outlawing of the secondary boycott, the Building Trades Department of the AFL-CIO and building trades councils throughout the land sometimes consider themselves fortunate to function as well as they do in commercial, industrial, and governmental building projects.

There is no doubt that they have a constant fight to maintain the security of their respective bargaining tables, let alone work out peacefully whose work belongs in whose jurisdiction on the major commercial jobs.

In-House Maintenance "Constructors"

Another area that constantly threatens the standards set at the bargaining table is the in-house construction of major employers. The battle goes on incessantly to achieve a basic objective of the building trades, to define clearly what is maintenance and what is construction.

In public buildings, unorganized workers often do both skilled and handyman types of maintenance. If an interior of a section of a building is to be remodeled, does the owner bring in an outside contractor to do the work? If so, is he union? In big plants, workers who belong to industrial unions have skilled classifications and often do major renovation on company payroll. Again, the building trades want guidelines so that the construction contractor brings in his work crew from the outside.

Guidelines have been and are being set in an increasing number of cases. For instance, a state might agree that any remodeling or renovation that involves over $10,000 of new material and labor time will not be done by the members of the maintenance crew, who are probably employees of the state and may carry craft union cards in good standing. Above that estimate of cost, the state puts the project up for bid. If it also has laws on prevailing conditions, the chances are that even a small job will be sublet to a private union contracting firm.

In the case of heavy industry, sophisticated arrangements of policy have been made among the local industrial union, the local plant management, the local building trades council, and the local contracting industry. For instance, in a steel plant, the company might agree that (1) any type of replacement construction (changing use or modernization of a site on which buildings are already situated) or

(2) any expansion of plant by construction of new facilities within the industrial plant complex will be done by bid contract, following prevailing conditions in the area. Thus, the building trades craftsman protects his right to do that job.

On the other hand, there are often major renovations of an identical pattern that have to be done at the same site within one or more of the plant buildings on a routine and regular operating basis. It can be agreed that the brick masons and ironworkers, for instance, who might be involved in this continuing renovation will be the same brick masons and ironworkers who make up the regular skilled maintenance crew.

In the light of public scrutiny, especially in recent years when construction has taken on major proportions in the United States, the building trades are accused of being unruly and too tough—treating the nonunion tradesman and his employer to unnecessary site picketing and occasional physical encounters. If all the construction contractors in the nation were union, it would cease; of course, all aren't, and until the American pattern changes, all won't be.

The building tradesman who is the committed and honest leader of his own craft jurisdiction or local union is not going to back down from anyone. He is usually as intensely loyal to his union as to his skill and craft; he sees the two as the same entity.

The Placing of the Picket—the "Situs"

Lastly, and very much related to the bargaining table, what the economically disadvantaged farm worker has going for him, the economically advantaged construction worker does not. He'd like to put extra teeth into the enforcement of that union contract under which he works—general or sub. He knows he could do it better by a picket line at the place where it ought to be—on any total job on which any craft is at work. The effect of outlawing the secondary boycott is that he cannot legally do so. He wants that picket where the site is—"situs picketing."

Even the workers' great favorite, Lyndon Baines Johnson, made no strong move to aid a heavily Democratic Congress to legalize situs picketing. Additionally, even though George Meany and his legislative spokesman, Andrew Biemiller, once a congressman from Milwaukee, had situs picketing on the AFL-CIO agenda in 1965 (and other years), the top priority was given to the repeal of RTW's special legal angle, 14(b).

The latter measure moved through the House of Representatives.

It had more than a majority on its side in the Senate. The filibustering open shop Senators, though, maintained more than the one-third vote they needed over a period of many weeks.

The repeal of 14(b) died.

In the interim, situs picketing didn't move through either house, and labor's political push failed in the 89th Congress. Situs picketing had been left pretty much to the Building Trades Department and councils. In the 1970s, the initiative has waned; the need is still urgent, but the political spirit is not so willing.

The building trades thus cannot place a picket anywhere except on the actual job site. If the dispute is with a general contractor, picketing can be only at a prime site. If that general contractor has a paving contractor five miles away on the same job, the building trades can't picket that subcontractor.

On the other hand, if a subcontractor is nonunion and the general contractor and/or other subcontractors are union, the building trades cannot picket every job site that relates to the overall construction job to which the nonunion subcontractor is contributing his defined share. If the subcontractor is electrical, for instance, the electricians can picket the site, but if the site is not near the point where the carpenter, engineer, cement mason, sheet metal worker, or any other craftsman or laborer is going to work, the picket doesn't halt the other crafts. If there is any one segment of the labor movement that understands the meaning of a picket on a person-to-person basis, it is the journeyman craftsman. At least, he matches the industrial worker who knows that he cannot go to work unless a whole plant shift goes to work.

The other crafts continue their work and can't even walk out of journeyman craftsman. At least, he matches the industrial worker who crossing the picket line and going to their own work.

A Type of Secondary Boycott

Situs picketing is the special term that relates to secondary boycott—except that the building trades want to use the picket in a more limited way than the way the industrial and retail trades unions could use the picket if the secondary boycott were as legal as it is in the rest of the Western world.

Situs picketing would be used on the same sites that the general contract jobs use. This would be especially true in the world of highways and multibuilding construction sites. Situs picketing could be used on the same general contractor at another site where he has a job, it is true, but if he is unfair on one site, the chances are he is unfair on the other, too. Situs picketing doesn't carry added significance in that event.

In an area like food distribution—from grower to processor to distributor to wholesaler to retailer—a legalized secondary boycott to the meatcutter or retail clerk could put the picket sign all the way back at the grower's gate.

Situs picketing is a special request to legalize a part of this process on the basis that all building crafts and all union contractors have their eggs in the same basket. The contention is that both sides of the bargaining table should stand united against nonunion contractors and nonunion workers.

BARGAINING IN THE PUBLIC SECTOR

It's a new thesis.

It's a new practice.

With some exceptions, public employees—those on payrolls of government—just didn't bargain prior to 1960. It was difficult to convince even their union leaders that they should try. The leaders within the public sector who tried to advance the theme seldom had a majority ear hearkening to them.

A new day is dawning. There is still a long way to get the sun high in the heavens. But most public employees agree that they have accepted their second-class citizenship for too long. Jerry Wurf had a hand in changing the pitch in the nonfederal employment. He now heads the rapidly growing American Federation of State, County and Municipal Employees, AFL-CIO (AFSCME).

New York Teachers Made the First Move

The old New York Teachers Guild made the first significant turning of the corner. They became convinced by persons like this author that public employees and the American Federation of Teachers (AFT), AFL-CIO, in particular, should not affiliate with trade unions unless their own union tried to bargain and sign agreements. They determined they could face the unpopular "public employees cannot strike" dictum en route to achieving the bargained contract.

Federal employees, especially the older and relatively strong National Association of Letter Carriers (NALC), were strong in terms of majority organization in the nation, and newer and younger mav-

ericks in some segments of the Postal Clerks—now American Postal
Workers Union (APWU)—received help. They were assisted by
President Jack Kennedy, Secretary of Labor Arthur Goldberg, his
special assistant Patrick Moynihan of Harvard fame, and some AFL-
CIO staffers.

President Kennedy had Goldberg send the Moynihan team around
the country to hear public and federal employee opinion on "what
kind of bargaining rights, if any" federal civilian employees should
have. As a result, the President issued an executive order recognizing
three kinds of union or employee associations plus the open shop and
the limited right to bargain at national, regional, and local levels of
federal employment.

The limited right did not permit much interference with civil
service rule-making authority or the establishment of grades of pay
or the assignment of job classifications to congressionally approved
pay grades. But it did give federal employee unions an opportunity
to set down some agreements in writing if the unions had sufficient
membership to achieve "exclusive" representation. Further, the agreements could include key grievance areas and job bidding guidelines
with a grievance processing procedure to provide union representation
in resolving complaints.

On another level, the New York teachers, through a merged and
larger AFT unit, became the United Federation of Teachers, AFT
Local 2. Local 2 won two elections following threats of strikes against
the New York Board of Education. It then bargained a contract.
Through the 1960s it secured working conditions generally superior
to any that teachers have anywhere in America.

Where it is better, in part at least, teachers in the big cities have
found the UFT Local 2 way a good way to go—and most of them
have had to strike for more than one or two days before finally
securing what they were seeking.

State Laws Beginning to Govern

The combination of these AFT successes from the Twin Cities to
Boston, along with some AFSCME contracts in major Eastern cities,
led to coincidental AFT/AFSCME support in state legislative lobbies.
They have brought recognition and bargaining rights by law to some
states—in New England, Pennsylvania, Michigan, Wisconsin, and
Hawaii. I use the word *coincidental* advisedly because there is no
love lost between the president of AFSCME, Jerry Wurf, and the
chief name known among the teacher unionists, Albert Shanker.

Shanker has been head of UFT since he sent his predecessor, Charles Cogen (now retired), off to head the AFT in Washington, D.C. The man who stood with them both, David Selden, who came from Dearborn to New York to help fashion the New York teachers' victory, has been president of the AFT in the 1970s, in name at least. Shanker has preempted behind the scenes on many occasions. In August, 1974, he handily unseated Selden as AFT president. He had already worked his way around both Selden and Wurf to join the AFL-CIO Executive Council at the 10th (October 1973) convention.

Meanwhile, Wurf has been pushing a public employee coalition for a national labor law for public employees—a labor law separate from NLRA—and wooing certain National Education Association (NEA) leaders in the process of supposedly formulating joint positions. This makes more complicated the efforts by Shanker to effect a merger of the NEA, which has been more of a professional association than a union, with the AFT. Shanker has already succeeded in merging NEA and AFT on equal bases across the state of New York —the home of both of these union presidents.

Shanker has gone through stages of very deliberate and carefully worded change as to how a merger of teacher organizations should occur to give them the largest single bargaining union in the nation —"teacher unity." But he is playing against Wurf's coalition. He has said the same to Selden—"You can't have it both ways"—inside and outside the AFL-CIO.

Shanker would contend it has something to do with how strong the "unified teachers" bargaining table is going to be—but for the moment, he sits on the delegate bodies in the "company-oriented" NEA and simultaneously at the right hand of George Meany as he counsels with the heads of labor.

Out of it all, regardless of his personal ambitions, Shanker may bring the NEA into the AFL-CIO, and a new name might be on the bargaining table at the same time—neither AFT nor NEA.

Federal Unions Growing Fast

The federal unions have grown by leaps and bounds.

Under Nixon's Jim Hodgson, the Department of Labor revised for the better at least one aspect of the executive order that permits limited rights to bargain. The Nixon order revoked the illogical three levels of recognition. It recognizes only one organization as the sole bargaining agent at each level where units can be defined. But the real issue is whether to bargain for wages or to replace the bureaucracy of civil service—and this is just where Arthur Goldberg left it, literally nowhere!

ALL THE OTHER UNIONS

It is not that they are lesser. Each in its own way fills a special niche in the American economy.

But in many cases, they are unions in limited areas of employment. In many other cases, they are unions that deal with almost monopoly business. In most cases, they deal in highly transient labor markets and have but a small percentage of the whole marketplace organized.

I don't expect all the names that follow to be read. Unless one is a reader of the Department of Labor's "Directory of National and International Labor Unions" or the AFL-CIO in-house listing of all of its affiliated bodies and departments, it is astounding to see the multiplicity of union jurisdictions that we still have, even though over two dozen unions of some name or significance have been merged with others in the 15 years preceding 1974. The appendix contains a complete list.

Looking at these seemingly interminable listings, a person can see in the names almost the apparent reason for any of these labor organizations. Additionally, they suggest diversity of interest—employers' and workers'—at a multitude of bargaining tables.

In the long list of independent unions, there are many relatively small organizations. They are small because the work force is small nationally or geographically. There are some substantially influential unions in their spheres, however. These include the Locomotive Engineers (about half of the nation's railroad engineers are here; the others are in UTU; in both instances, each bargains contracts across total rail systems and not in competition with each other); National Postal Union (which has the New York City Post Office, among others); the Rural Letter Carriers; the competing general federal employee unions (AFGE is AFL-CIO), NAGE and NFFE; and the various professional sports labor organizations.

Before leaving this description of labor as bargainer, I should reemphasize the multiplicity of unions, the occasional overlap of jurisdictions, and the inevitable tens of thousands of contracts that are up for local union bargaining each year.

Additionally, several more unions ought to be picked out for special attention in this type of overview—even though it is not the purpose of this book to go into great detail on any one union, bargaining pattern, or case example.

CWA Faces Ma Bell

In the industrial union area, one of the newest and now one of the largest (formerly the independent telephone workers) is the AFL-CIO affiliate, Communications Workers of America (CWA). This union has dabbled in various kinds of union organizing, even outside of what might be called its normal jurisdiction. Primarily, however, it is what its name implies. And in the world of our country's communications, the basic person-to-person communicator is the telephone system.

Although there are still several score independent telephone companies—some with growing subscriber lists (as in Las Vegas, Nevada, where there are more telephones than people but occasionally less service)—it is safe to say that 80 percent of the nation's business is in 22 regional systems, all subsidiaries of the company known affectionately, or not so affectionately, as Ma Bell.

American Telephone and Telegraph Company, the Bell System, is interlocked in its communications with its equipment supplier, Western Electric. Over the Bell System, including Western Electric, the chances are that the operations are under contract with CWA. In some areas, CWA is union shop. In some, it has recently gained the agency shop (all eligible workers pay the fee, but there is no membership requirement). In some of its regional operations, it is open shop.

Where CWA is open shop, the principal workers who normally do not belong are the long distance operators. There are local operators, too, primarily for assistance calls. The outside linemen, service repair crews, installer repairmen, and the like usually band together. The open part of the shop also generally extends to the Bell System's offices—business and service.

Even though Bell is now employing some men in the former open shop world of women (offices, switchboards, and the like) and some women in the former skilled blue-collar journeymen areas of work assignment (plant), it's the jobs in these predominantly female areas of employment that are on the lower end of the scale and pay rates. The men's world of work is proportionately higher paid under the terms of the company-union agreement.

If CWA could wrap up the entire communications industry of America, it would still have trouble enforcing its demands in typical classifications of work. CWA's jurisdiction is a computerized world. When a strike occurs, the automated world of Bell and Western Electric continues to operate for days before the equipment finally begins to jam and otherwise fail. Bell, as the monopoly franchise operator in most localities of the U.S., can take a strike easier than any multibillion-dollar giant. It can afford to rest instead of hiring scabs in the initial days of the strike. This has an effect on the final settlements.

It should be noted that CWA is not the sole bargainer with AT&T. In some unit areas, IBEW has Bell contracts. With Western Electric as manufacturer, as contrasted with supplier and operator, IBEW has a substantial share of the local plants, (but not on the same sites as CWA). Western Electric has varying union patterns, therefore—the bargaining is with the local union having jurisdiction at the plant site. By the same token, CWA, with master agreements covering the big communicator, does not have the same terms in the Southern Bell contract as in the Northwest Bell contract.

Printing Trades

The oldest union in North America is the ITU (International Typographical Union), formerly headquartered where many key unions were for years—Indianapolis (which used to be considered the center of the nation's population). In the early '60s, the union moved its headquarters to a modern, multimillion-dollar plant on prime property that it has held for years, looking from a high ground vantage west across Colorado Springs directly on Pikes Peak.

The street where ITU lives has been for years called Union Boulevard; part of the property has been occupied since the late nineteeenth century by the first Medicare institution in the land—the Printers' Home of the ITU. In addition to the home and new head-quarters, one of the most modern and experimental vocational training institutions in the world occupies a nearby site—the ITU Training Center, which is worth anyone's visit.

ITU embraces printers. Dating back into the 1950s, its officers had mapped out plans for the logical amalgamation or merger of the various crafts in the printing industry—pressmen, photoengravers, stereotypers, lithographers, bookbinders. The name that the late Elmer Brown, then president of ITU, talked about was Graphic Arts.

Another Brown, Kenneth (no relative, but with an outlook and vision similar to Elmer Brown's), has taken the key to ITU's discussion and put three of the printing trades unions under one roof: Graphic Arts Union.

In September, 1972, the Bookbinders merged with the formerly merged Lithographers and Photoengravers. The Lithographers had been the former CIO union which had organized in some plants on an industrial basis—had agreed to take the paste up and photo-offset process under its own jurisdiction and contribute to higher speed printing processes.

The old processes of reproducing pictures and drawings on the printing presses included the cutting, or etching, of metal plates—the photoengravers were a small but distinguished craft performing that service. The Lithos pasted up pictures and proofs of typeset and made up a total plate of a page or pages—not just a single picture. Thus the "total printer" and the "single cut" (picture) photoengraver put their industrial type and craft union together first—then later added the bookbinders.

They have now become three-in-one under the Graphic Arts label.

In the meantime, the Pressmen, the craft that runs and maintains the printing presses, moved to compete and set up separate locals in big cities in the last several decades to do what the Lithos were doing—offset, high-speed printing. In 1973, the Stereotypers cast their lot with the Pressmen.

Also in the printing and publishing trades is the Newspaper Guild—the writers, particularly in the news and periodical publication fields. On the big city newspapers, the Guild organizes every workers' classification except the printers, pressmen, and binders. They are the industrial union of the newspaper business—industrial except in the mechanical shops that turn out the printed product.

A vast number of small and large, good and bad duplicating and offset-type printing shops have entered the field. The apprenticeable printing trades all consider the cheap printing processes—with their mediocre-quality reproduction and low-paid, easy-to-train mechanics and other personnel—as a threat to all publishing business.

ITU, at the top of the printing crafts in working conditions and laws, has been able to hold onto its standards and upgrade its craft, even though it has not become the instrument of merger for one graphic arts union. In 1974, the leadership of ITU and Pressmen, each larger than Graphic Arts, made a move toward merger—hopefully total merger that will include what Ken Brown has already accomplished in preliminary mergers.

Allied Printing Trades Emblem—One Union Purpose

The key union emblem to the printing trades unions is the joint label that says that all of their respective crafts or jurisdictions are in the shop that has done the publishing. The symbol of the union shop agreement is the Allied Printing Trades Label. Allied Printing Trades councils are located in every major city of America. They are found in most daily newspaper shops and in the larger commercial printing shops, either general or specialty, in most cities.

The unilaterally apprenticeable printing crafts have not drawn many publishing or printing houses into jointly sharing the responsibilities of apprentice training—that is, they do usually not have under either federal or state registration programs for apprentices, the so-called "joint registration."

But the printers (typographers) in particular and the pressmen, engravers, stereotypers, electrotypers, and the other crafts of old have carefully formulated their own on-the-job training programs to bring the newly hired craftsman along the route from apprentice to journeyman.

Like the building trades, they did not sign agreements in many instances before NLRA was enacted in 1935, and so they built laws and procedures into their own standards of work. They also set up health and retirement programs from the dues and assessments paid by each member each month. As a result, both the printers and the pressmen have very extensive, carefully invested retirement plans. They both operate retirement homes with medical and recreational facilities attached to the complete living facilities.

The ITU Training Center (and the Pressmen have one of their own, too) is operated on the pragmatic understanding that workers need to get off the job from time to time to review what they are doing, how they are doing it, and what new techniques and new equipment might be utilized. Even the long-term journeyman needs to adapt and increase his proficiency.

ITU's Center—Key to Jobs and Bargaining

ITU has been able to obtain staff out of its own ranks, who not only become excellent teachers but who have been able to invent many parts of the new computerized printing machines.

The advantage of the latter is with ITU. When it bargains and faces potential layoffs because of an exotic piece of equipment that reduces manpower needs (for instance, electronic tape typesetting of the same story simultaneously in any city newsroom possessing the equipment), ITU can put its own patented invention on the bargaining table as a means of making certain that the member is not laid off. It has the bargaining strength to secure placement for him elsewhere in new production facilities of the same employer.

Known by some as a conservative union, ITU is in fact highly progressive in terms of representing its own members with solid support at the bargaining table. It is a union that cares for its members— not in the welfare sense, but in the positive sense of aiding the member to upgrade his own work abilities and creativity while securing his continuing employment and his security in retirement.

The printing trades know that they have not only members' rights to protect but employers' economic well-being in a world that is turning out more printed words than any comparable decade in our history. The unions at the bargaining table are willing to keep pace with the increasing volume—newspapers, paperbacks, high-speed, multicolored press runs of periodicals and books, posters and advertising layouts—but they feel that the work week can be cut still further to keep employment up without decreasing profitable operations as the work unit of production increases so rapidly.

Significantly, this one historical item is a good conclusion to this chapter. It was the ITU and the printing trades, as craftsmen, who organized and aided the Committee on Industrial Organization in the A.F. of L. of the 1920s. They realized that all workers stand to lose unless all workers—skilled and unskilled—can organize.

4

Labor's Diversities

The elements of this chapter are rooted in those of the preceding chapter. That is to say, the diversities that face unions and managements at the bargaining table have caused the multitude of differences that exist among national and international unions. Additionally, the diversity reaches into the areas of autonomy that local unions have maintained.

There is diversity in the many kinds of American unions, which, even at that, still do not provide "houses" or jurisidictions for millions of American workers who could or would seek unionization.

There is diversity in the variety of sizes of unions—locally and nationally.

But most of all, I want to discuss in this chapter the diversity of the institution that calls itself free in the structure of "representative democracy." Even in those unions where democratic processes are called for in the constitution, undemocratic processes are followed.

Worker Involvement Requires Democracy in Workplace

It all depends on how one wants to look at it, of course, but not too many American unions can back up their assertions of democratic operations and structures. Each is able to be much more democratic than it is.

The hope of American labor rests on the involvement of the worker in the democracy of the workplace. His own special voice needs analysis if it is to be constantly upgraded to serve his own best needs at work as well as in the political, social, and economic community at large.

The constant assertion of autonomy by the leaders of America's many unions, probably more than any other single reason, accounts for the fact that American labor really is a less cohesive movement than it could be. If there is a trait of selfishness in any of us who have achieved elected leadership status, it is best exhibited in the unwillingness to relinquish any prerogatives either to anyone peering up from the vertical structure of one's own union or leaning in too close from the side. The latter relates to the unions that stand vertically on either side of a union, extending arms to help each other as part of the movement.

Diversity has meant the extremely loose confederation known as the AFL-CIO. Diversity has permitted the Auto Workers and Teamsters to flourish without apparently needing anyone else.

Less Than the Spirit of "Solidarity Forever"

The spirit of autonomy is not just one of independence; it is one that preserves such authority as one has unto oneself. It is less than the spirit of the song of the movement, "Solidarity Forever." It is a spirit of saying within the House of Labor that the individual "states" take precedence over the "nation."

This is not necessarily bad, though it makes it difficult to pull labor leaders together on the many occasions when the country would be better off if they were more closely knit.

There is kind of a nationalistic spirit within the separate jurisdictions of most trade unions. This chauvinism doesn't build the element of sharing to a high pitch; it tends to emphasize that sharing is only for the selected few who happen to belong to "our own union." The spirit of "to each his own" has probably impeded labor's growth, involvement, strength, and democratic progress more than any single factor.

Of course, the diverse business pursuits developed over the years in the American economy have contributed to labor's diversity. Unions have adapted themselves to the business establishment. Labor has even adopted the smugness of the business and professional society that regards the white-collar worker as different from the blue-collar worker. There is no unity implied in the phrase, "A worker is a worker." There is none of the feeling that "Any person who draws a paycheck from a nonfamily employer needs a union as much as any other person who draws a paycheck—white, black, brown, red, yellow—skin color or collar color."

Leaving out the White Collar

Unions' diversities have been mostly among blue-collar workers; the white-collar worker has been left out in a very major way, for mainly faulty if not false reasoning.

Unions are big where the workplace is big. Business is big in the same locations. Unions are smaller where the highly skilled positions are still extracted out of the total work force in separate units and where high skills are not demanded of a multitude of workers in the same workplace. Thus, the skill classifications still maintain an often artificial diversity in trade unionism.

"Who belongs in my house?" continues to be the question. The overtones of the question smack of snobbishness, but it has rubbed off from craft unions to the industrial unions. As some grizzled and gritty industrial workers—not their leaders—would put it, "Steelworkers go first class!"

What's good for the craftsman is good for the worker. Isn't the craftsman a worker? At least, it is a way of speaking up while saying, "I'm as good as you are, but I'll stay in my house and you stay in yours!"

A Shared Commodity: Maintaining Union Security

As already mentioned, the one place of broad sharing of understanding from one separate union to the other is union security. "If you attack someone else's union security, you are attacking mine." But for unity to occur, the attack has to be clear-cut and well defined, like proposing a compulsory open shop.

American labor has been not quite willing to put aside its many differences in job classifications, working conditions, economic benefits, health and safety conditions, and employers' operations for the simple, shared purpose of obtaining union security for all who work for a living. The individual, vertical union structures have not been weakened enough over the years by either internal or external pressures to lead them to that conclusion.

Leadership not Pressed to Take Down Fences

Accordingly, the elected leaders at the top of these separatist structures have, with few exceptions, not pressed for moving horizontally—taking down the fences between themselves and their neighbors. In the process, of course, they would have to give up leadership, in the manner of sacrifice that Walter Reuther did in favor of George Meany in 1955 when "two houses became one."

Jerry Wurf (AFSCME) has been rumbling louder each year about paring down the 115 unions we still have to a more logical 25 to 30 unions——so "we can stand our ground better against our enemies." (And also hopefully organize the unorganized, who have so few places to turn in seeking better answers to their own economic disadvantages.)

If Walter Reuther were alive, he would probably be preaching the same sermon. The late Joe Bierne (CWA) probably had it in his new leadership program when it appeared he could be a successor to George Meany if Walter Reuther were not to be. And there are hundreds of leaders, just below the top positions of their own unions, who look favorably on unity, too—although it might interfere with their own respective ascendencies. Why risk disfavor from those who might give one's rope an upward pull someday?

Does the system interefere with merging labor's diversities into a united House of Labor? Does the institutional structure? Do the separatist pronouncements of autonomy? Yes, they do!

We examine the diversities in labor democracy existing now in the various unions. In the final chapter, we prognosticate about spreading democracy through the sorely needed horizontal studding that it seems to me will have to be built into the House of Labor before the mid-'80s.

Landrum-Griffin: Political Compromise

The Landrum-Griffin amendments to the National Labor Relations Act and the National Railway Labor Act came at the end of the Eisenhower years but out of a Democratic Congress. They were the end result of compromise between the vindictiveness of the anti-labor forces (for whom Landrum and Griffin provided sponsorship) that were doing more than was warranted by what had been revealed by the McClellan Committee and the Bobby Kennedy prosecution of the committee's case against Jimmy Hoffa, on the one hand, and the political sensitivity of prolabor senators like Jack Kennedy and Hubert Humphrey.

The amendments that relate most directly to the diversities in trade union structures dealt with declared federal interest in the right of the union member as an individual to be protected within his union. The proposal was reduced, primarily, to the relationship of the individual member of his immediate union—his local union— after the labor lobbies and the Kennedys and the Humphreys agreed on revisions that softened the intent of the Landrums and the Griffins.

Among the proposals that dealt with the constitutional structures of all unions were the length of terms of union offices; the frequency with which national and international unions must convene delegate bodies; the use of the secret ballot in electing local union officers and local union delegates to conventions or delegate conferences of the parent union; and the recourse that the individual members had to secure their rights through the intervention defined for federal agencies within the Department of Labor.

Labor in the late '50s felt certain that business interests would put individual employees up to harassing local unions through filings with Labor Department offices. Some of this did develop—and some developed from members' own initiatives—but the harassment has not been severe.

Variations in Union Procedures

Just what are the processes that differ among American unions? Most of them were not in fact required to change constitutions or bylaws to comply with the new additions to labor law—the local and international union constitutions were stronger in the definition and protection of individual union member's rights than Landrum-Griffin.

Some unions have provisions that invest rather heavy authority in a select group of elected officers—usually called executive councils or executive boards. The size of the council varies with the union and does not necessarily parallel the size of the union's membership. Some large unions have boards of less than a dozen persons; some small unions have boards in excess of two dozen. The average size runs around 16.

Although councils may be principally or entirely full-time officers, most of them are not so constituted. However, full-time officers are relied upon for leadership and direction. Councils meet as infrequently as semiannually and as frequently as monthly or even on shorter call.

The full-time officers of unions vary from one to as many as ten in number. Generally, the chief officer is the president, though sometimes it is the secretary-treasurer (a hangover from the craft union days where the fiscal officer was considered the key to the union's survival).

Most unions with more than 50,000 members (and this is most of the unions in the U. S.) have at least two full-time officers with constitutionally divided responsibilities—one primarily to lead, persuade, speak, and guide (the president), the other to make certain the union maintains fiscal responsibility, administrative efficiency, and housekeeping (secretary-treasurer or financial secretary).

Authority over Local Unions

The chief variances among unions are in the constitutional authority vested in the basic national or international organizations. Some
unions exercise tight supervision over their local unions. As a result,
trusteeships are not uncommon. Most union officers at the top level
seem simultaneously to decry and to enjoy that authority—the power
of discipline that keeps the echelons in line, so to speak. This is the
love-hate personality that autocratic leadership and stardom often
develop in a person. A few do not like the power and do not use it
unless fiscal corruption is proved at the local union level.

Although a big union like UAW has strong policy control from
the top down, it does have conventions every two years where both
policy and control can be effectively tempered; additionally, it has
established a third-party public review board composed of persons
having no connection with UAW and of high public repute. This
board can receive and act upon any grievance of any member against
any local, district, or international union officer. It is the "assurance
of democratic privilege to which every individual is to have equal
and unfettered access" that matches the sermons of Walter Reuther
and his UAW colleagues over the years.

Some unions do not even have the power of trusteeship over
local unions that they charter. Usually, however, most unions do
provide for suspension or even revocation of charters of local unions
for violating constitutional principles of the parent union.

In-House Appeal Structure

All charter revocations are subject to appeal. The first appeal is
inevitably to the authority within the union that made the decision
to suspend or revoke—usually the executive board or council of the
parent union.

The next appeal step is a little more open in the national or
international union structure—to the next convention of the union.
But when conventions are held only once in three, four, or five years,
it could be a long wait—and in the case of the AFL-CIO itself, as well
as many of its affiliate unions, the conventions are closely controlled
by ranking delegates of the larger affiliate bodies. Usually these
ranking delegates are also the members of the executive council.

The appendix of this book offers a contemporary case in point
dealing with the AFL-CIO process. Many national unions have similar open ballot systems. Since most conventions are in the same kind
of control situation, they rule on appeals from local unions in about

the same manner—that is, sustaining the position of the governing officers of the union who made the decision.

The American Federation of Teachers, without trustee authority, has a public review board. AFT has given it no consitutional authority, however, and many local leaders like Shanker of New York would never agree to an individual member's right to petition the board or to a local union's petition against the AFT national officers. The board, which started with fanfare and such prominent labor arbitrators as Ted Kheel and John Philip Linn on deck, became an appendage of no consequence in a few years.

Secret Ballot—To Which Offices Shall It Apply?

The secret ballot does not reach up to the top circles of labor very often. Whenever any local member or leader, let alone national leader, proposes that all offices within the union be subject to a secret ballot of all eligible members, most unions have a way of agreeing how impossible such a situation would be. The issue is then defeated in a lightly voted mail ballot referendum or in the next open ballot convention of the same union.

Two unions of prominence in American labor have proved that the arguments against electing national and local officers by the secret ballot are more myth than fact. These two unions of different sizes and economic and cultural constituencies both cherish and exercise their respective rights of franchise. One is the largest union in the AFL-CIO—the United Steelworkers of America, with over one million members in the United States and Canada. The other is the nation's oldest, the International Typographical Union, with over 120,000 members in the United States and Canada.

Both unions elect all of their officers locally, at the district (multistate in some cases) level, and at the international union level by secret ballot. Every member is entitled to vote, and substantial majorities exercise that franchise.

The mood of the American labor movement might change if every union officer were subject to what USWA and ITU find acceptable, strengthening practices. The structures of vertical and parallel unionism might also be changed in the process because of the leadership selection process and what the potential leaders might then dare to do.

Conventions: The Highest Authority

Conventions are usually considered the highest authority within each union's structure. Under federal law, if not under constitutional requirements of each union, convention delegates must be chosen by secret ballot, if the union bargains at any level in the private sector of the country. Since most unions do bargain with private business, the secret ballot is usually required. Moreover, the Landrum-Griffin amendments provide that notice in writing must reach every member at a defined period of time prior to the election.

While some unions elect by referendum ballot or by membership polling places, most unions elect their officers and delegates at local union meetings. Meetings are not well attended—never have been, even before the advent of affluence, television, and a multitude of other outside attractions. Even with the secret ballot, local union leaders can usually find ways to persuade the members whom they want to be present. Secret ballot or not, unless a major revolt is brewing—and for the health of the movement at local union levels, there is always a potential brew—the convention delegates elected at the meeting normally are those "who count." And if the local union leader is ambitious and wants to gain favor with the international officers or their representatives, the chances are good that the officers chosen in that convention to direct the parent union for another three, four, or five years will have their supporters in the convention hall on election day.

Most convention ballots are open, not secret. The proposition is simple: the delegates from each local have to show the members back home that they voted as the members desired. The open ballot shows whom the delegates supported.

The argument that I, among others, make against this system is that while an open vote on a controversial issue is necessary, a secret ballot vote for a person is also necessary. Otherwise, the person who might make a better officer—but has not been selected to be in the open ballot slate by the local unions that together have a majority of the delegate strength of the convention—is defeated in spite of the merit of his candidacy. The delegate has the opportunity to see and hear the candidates firsthand. His vote could be subject to control in an open ballot. His vote is honest and uncontrolled in a secret ballot.

Variable Patterns in Frequency of Conventions

The convention structures of American labor include a timeless factor that says something about how to structure and control the representative assembly, as often as not with a minimum rather than a maximum of democratic guarantees and input. Here is the frequency schedule, as of 1973, of the conventions of all of the 115 AFL-CIO and 62 independent labor organizations required under Landrum-Griffin to register with the Department of Labor's annual reporting system:

One small union meets quarterly; two small unions meet semi-annually; two small unions meet upon call; 32 meet annually, including CWA, ITU, and AFT; the greatest number, 64, meets each two years, including the Steelworkers, Bricklayers, AFSCME, and Wood-workers; 20 meet every three years; 37 meet only once in four years, including such diverse types as TWU, Textile, UTU (operating railroad brotherhoods), Carpenters and IBEW (the two largest in the construction industry), Iron Workers, Machinists (one of the five largest in the AFL-CIO), Meat Cutters, Retail Clerks, Sheet Metal Workers, and Service Employees; and 19 meet every fifth year including the nation's largest, the Teamsters, and one of the top building crafts, the United Association (plumbers and fitters), along with the Molders, Laborers, Painters, Locomotive Engineers, Railway Carmen, and Hotel-Restaurant-Bartenders.

The diversity of structure and operation has something to do with the strength of membership involvement permitted—the degree of democracy allowed—and is the result of two factors: the variables in the workplace and the creation of structures aimed at preserving if not creating diversity in union operations.

5

Caught in the Middle

As the clearing house for the labor movement, the AFL-CIO has devised in its structure a carry-over from both of its predecessor organizations—but primarily from the old A.F. of L. format.

Local unions within a state that are chartered by any AFL-CIO union may also affiliate with a state central body, which itself is an affiliate of the AFL-CIO. Local central bodies, dealt with briefly in the next chapter, are similar kinds of creatures and affiliates of the AFL-CIO.

Accordingly, any local AFL-CIO union can belong to its national/ international union, to its state AFL-CIO, and to its local AFL-CIO. It can affiliate with a local or statewide council just as its parent union affiliates with the AFL-CIO at the national level.

There are several basic differences, however. The principal one is that the local union of an AFL-CIO affiliate does not have to join any state or local central body. The AFL-CIO exercises no element of compulsion for it to do so. It has committees; it has passed resolutions; it has a coordinating office within its department of organization— but that's about as close as the AFL-CIO gets to the matter of even urging unions to affiliate their memberships at the state and local levels.

Probably the AFL-CIO itself does not quite receive a full membership count and payment from many of its own affiliates. The approximately 13,400,000 per capita units paid to it at the end of 1973 was within 600,000 of the probably 14,000,000 members that its national and international unions had in the United States.

The aggregate affiliate per capita payments in the 50 State bodies have never reached the 8,000,000 figure. State leaders decry this loudly enough to be heard but not seriously listened to. Some states have managed to get to a 70 percent affiliate status in per capita units of all AFL-CIO members in their respective states. If all did, even that would show a total of fewer than 9,800,000 across the nation.

The open shop—which all trade unionists abhor—is (1) the practice of the AFL-CIO affiliate local unions and (2) the policy of their respective national and international union leadership in most cases.

In some states, the AFL-CIO national union that has the average of the worst local union affiliate status across the nation—less than 40 percent of its membership in state central bodies—has local unions with close to 100 percent affiliate status in some states. In contrast, the national AFL-CIO unions that have the best statewide overall averages (between 70 and 80 percent) have listings at 9 to 20 percent of their local union memberships in some states.

It is difficult to generalize about practices and trends. It just happens to be a problem at the state and local central body levels. Affiliation may depend upon state leadership, local union leadership, state program, or simply whim. Usually financial reasons are given when locals don't affiliate with either state or local central bodies.

The other differences are more real than constitutional.

What AFL-CIO Leadership Expects

The interpretation of the AFL-CIO leadership is basically one of saying to its central bodies, "Support our policies. We provide the guidelines. Excite local union membership through their leadership to support our policies. Do the best you can with your own state government. Elect pro-union people to the Congress. Do pretty much as we do. We'll give you most of the answers."

Since state leadership comes out of local union halls and is closer to the problems of the local unions than either the faraway AFL-CIO or the national and international union leaders in most cases, the state bodies really are more "rarin' to go" than the AFL-CIO is anxious for them to "go."

If the state leaders feel that they will be better treated at the top by not "going" too much, that's the way they will lead their respective state bodies. The state leaders may feel that they ought to be exerting their own leadership more strongly. But when the state body becomes more determined and aggressive, it may not be shown many favors by the AFL-CIO. (The latter half of this chapter offers a good case study of a state body that stood its ground in what some other state leaders might call ill-advised defiance of the AFL-CIO president. However, in the union halls, the membership remained considerably more understanding and supportive of the state body than its creator, the AFL-CIO.)

State Authority not Easily Definable

What is the state central body's authority? Generally, it is to be the spokesman for the AFL-CIO on matters that relate to AFL-CIO interests within the state. That is simple. It sounds as if it is easy and ought to be clearly definable.

State central bodies are caught in the middle, however. They find that general charge not so definable. In the organizational field, the state central bodies would like to aid in the organization of new workers, but they are not permitted to do so. That is the job of the respective national or international union with a jurisdictional interest in the state.

If the national unions fail to do their jobs, if they fail to support their own local union or unions in that job, then the job is not done or is only partially done. The state AFL-CIO leadership is helpless to aid in bringing workers into the mainstream of trade unionism. To persons who want the answers and request an explanation, this is puzzling. "Aren't you the AFL-CIO? We don't get it!"

If the trouble did stem from the AFL-CIO itself, the situation might be corrected more readily. The trouble goes back to the vertical union structures that will share only limited authority with the AFL-CIO.

Walter Reuther used to say that the separate unions would have to learn to bridge that gap—that logical organizational efforts would more readily stem from the House of Labor than from the individual jurisdictions. He never saw this come to pass. He tried to do it in 1968-1969 through the Alliance for Labor Action (ALA), which at one time drew four affiliate national unions, including the two largest— Teamsters and UAW—but his dreams and the Teamsters' operations weren't quite fitting together when he met his untimely death, so the ALA has not survived.

Meany's Attitude Limits State Bodies

George Meany, who came to the old A.F. of L. from the top office of the largest state central body, New York, has taken another approach. The state central body is to be active in legislative lobbying primarily and political action if necessary to be effective in the legislatures.

State central bodies usually have relatively large executive boards, which normally meet at least four times per year. They are large because of the need to get a representative cross section of the local union affiliates. The best way for most state central bodies to maintain at least a 50 percent per capita support from the AFL-CIO local unions is to have leaders from local unions whose total membership represents at least 50 percent of each state's AFL-CIO membership.

Often the state boards have members whose national or international unions compete in some of the same jurisdictions. This condition not only provides problems in the strength of the state body's own public voice, but it further weakens the opportunity of the state body to give even moral support to organizational efforts. Inevitably, the determination of the national and international unions to call their own shots influences the local unions. Even when local leadership resents and occasionally rebels against this domination, the independence of the state to speak for itself is still restricted.

Probably the reason that George Meany has been so well suited as leader of the merged labor federations since 1955 is because he has not dared to challenge the respective authorities of the affiliates. At the same time, he has spoken with more authority than he is constitutionally given in addressing the state and local central bodies that are uniquely under AFL-CIO sponsorship.

Unequal enforcement of rules by the AFL-CIO and its president is common and explainable, but it is considered unjust and frustrating by state leaders who do not want to overlook the potential of their organizations. One sore point is the unwillingness of President Meany or his staff to suspend the illegal affiliations of the Teamsters with building trades councils (formally chartered within the AFL-CIO) and food councils (not formally chartered). The AFL-CIO constitution is clear—the Teamsters do not belong because they have been disaffiliated by convention action.

At the state and local level, however, almost all the officers in the AFL-CIO central bodies would prefer that the Teamsters be a part of the AFL-CIO, Hoffa and Fitzsimmons notwithstanding. At the local levels, the leadership is looking at Teamsters' membership and leadership. Delivery trucks to the supermarkets and their warehouses are of mutual concern to the drivers, warehousemen, meatcutters, retail clerks, machinists, engineers, and others. Construction truck drivers are a key link in the building and construction craft union structures.

Thus, the illegal affiliations are untouched—almost blessed—and sometimes even build local political alliances that are not consistent with AFL-CIO Committee and Political Education (COPE) programs.

It all adds up to the questions that were asked in 1972 general election campaigns from the platforms of many state AFL-CIO COPE conventions, best expressed as one state officer in a large southern state put it: "Just who the hell does George Meany think he is?"

More appropriately, all the state officers know very well who President Meany is, how he operates, and what unequal treatment under AFL-CIO laws and rules means. More important, they also know it should all be revised, hopefully with the Teamsters and all unions in one House of Labor with authority to speak the democratic decisions of membership at each level out loud.

Still Caught in the Intermix

At this time, state bodies are caught in the intermix of: (1) the autocratic pronouncements of the AFL-CIO president; (2) the strong differences that still exist among the unions that have created the AFL-CIO; (3) the frustrations of local union leaders as they try to speak independently about their own state central body but find themselves hemmed in by their own international unions' desires not to let any part of the AFL-CIO get out of hand; and (4) the general public's belief that the state central body leadership should speak the mind of the labor leadership within its own state.

"So, what else is new?"

That's the response of anyone inside and outside labor who doesn't want to rock any boats. And it is thrown up to the state and local central body leaders who are willing to stand up and speak with candor about their roles in the AFL-CIO.

Differing Legislative Views of AFL-CIO Jurisdictions

It is true that state central bodies are supposed to be the one voice that speaks to state government—legislative and executive—about how labor views the problems affecting working people in the state. The AFL-CIO doesn't exercise much interference here; the structure occasionally interferes, however.

What happens in many states is that the building trades look at government one way; the railroad brotherhoods look at it another way; the industrial unions can't readily understand the postures of either of the former; and the miscellaneous trades have as many problems to confront public officials as they have unions.

With all the differing views, how does a state central body help to get a good public employee bargaining law on the books? The AFSCME locals want to be sure the law defines bargaining units to cut across craft lines. The building trades want to carve out units of their crafts who work in maintaining public buildings, roads, and properties. Teachers sometimes try to put "professional" definitions in the guidelines for a bargaining unit. The Fire Fighters union might opt only for definitions that do not damage provisions that it has established in home rule city charters. The welfare workers don't want to lose their attachment to federal subsidies of welfare departments.

If all the jurisdictions decide to bargain for separate exceptions and terms, the single state labor body's voice is silenced before it begins. It becomes extremely difficult to put together a common proposal to satisfy all. Most states, accordingly, do not have laws—and many states have punitive laws that outlaw public employees' right to strike. State central bodies have had difficulty dealing in this area of legislative activity.

When it comes to occupational safety and health (OSHA), there was a rebirth of labor interest in the early '70s. The AFL-CIO found that the only way it could get a wide-sweeping federal law passed and signed by the President in 1970 was if Congress provided that states which met federal standards could enforce the act's provisions at the state level.

The AFL-CIO then pressed the state central bodies to lobby against any plan or law that was designed to allow the state to enforce the provisions of OSHA. In many states, however, the building trades took the position that the state was closer to home and could more readily get enforcement authorities out to inspect the job sites. In other states, because of the political ties between some labor leaders and legislators, other jurisdictions believed the state was more appropriate as the enforcement agency.

The AFL-CIO kept promulgating the policies, and the state central bodies kept supporting the policies. Usually, the industrial unions were on the side of federal enforcement, too. But at the end of 1973, most states had approved plans and/or legislation for state enforcement of OSHA, and the state central bodies had to bear the brunt of the divisions in the ranks.

On the matter of equal rights for women—especially the efforts of many interests to hold off the ratification of the federal constitutional amendment by 38 states—local jurisdictions within states did not stand in the way of state central bodies supporting ratifications; the AFL-CIO did until October, 1973. Then, under great pressure from the growing women's membership in trade unions and the embarrassment caused among otherwise public allies (like the League of Women Voters), the AFL-CIO changed its posture. In the interim, there were some unnecessarily harsh criticisms in both directions as state councils found that some of their own members demanded their support of equal rights and that they were losing a certain amount of credibility with natural allies in the halls of the state legislatures.

These are examples that result from an unclear delegation of authority and no substantive backup from the AFL-CIO to its state central bodies.

Speaking with a Common Voice

About the only places, once again, where there is no dissent among trade unionists of all affiliations are in the fields of union security, workmen's compensation, and unemployment insurance benefits as defined by state governments. The state central body can, in these instances, speak with one voice even if it is not supported by the per capita revenues of all trade unions that are eligible to be a part of it.

Everyone wants the right to negotiate the union shop in contracts with employers. Everyone wants the model standards for workmen's compensation (job injury) benefits written into state laws. Everyone wants at least a two-thirds benefit of the average weekly pay for the worker who is out of work through no fault of his own and ready to work in any occupation for which he is qualified.

COPE

Where the state AFL-CIO is most caught in the middle is in the field of activity of COPE, the Committee on Political Education.

The state bodies are responsible for carrying on statewide programs among the families of the union members to inform them about the issues in Congress and in the state capitals that specifically affect the working person. The state bodies are also supposed to coordinate and provide programs aimed at getting the qualified adult members of union families registered and out to vote.

The state board is responsible for recommending candidates who are favorable to the best interests of trade unionists for the state legislature, statewide offices (like governor), and for the U.S. Congress.

Although this would seem to be clear-cut, the central AFL-CIO has a tendency to let its COPE and legislative department staff involve themselves in who ought to be in Congress. On occasion, this activity runs counter to the judgments of the people in the state offices. This is probably natural, since the lobbying activities in Congress are performed by the AFL-CIO legislative director and his staff. It is difficult to detach oneself from the representatives and senators with whom one has established good working relationships.

When some of these long-time congressional friends find themselves involved in primaries or general election battles with newcomers

—even newcomers who might be more friendly to labor—decisions are made at the AFL-CIO COPE level that may undercut the positions taken by the state bodies.

One of the contestants has to win in the primary balloting, but if it is not the AFL-CIO's old-time Washington friend, a coolness in terms of assisting the campaign of the newcomer often spells defeat for a campaign that might otherwise be won. Local unions that might otherwise help the state central body often feel the pressure from the top staff of their unions as a spinoff from the AFL-CIO COPE staff's attitude.

If COPE would fully observe what the rules say the state's position is, labor would fare better at the polling place. If the state errs, it can accept responsibility, because it's the AFL-CIO members in the state who will suffer the most. When AFL-CIO COPE interference helps to create the loss that should not happen, then the state body feels strongly that it has been caught in the middle.

State-Local Central Body Entanglements

Another way the state body suffers in AFL-CIO structure is the national office's unwillingness to define the posture of the local area central bodies as they relate to the state. The larger the local area, the easier it is for the local leadership to set up its own voice in making political recommendations for state legislative and congressional seats.

Since some of the members of the local central body are also members of the state central body, it would seem that the same local union leaders are speaking out twice. Often, however, local central bodies have few (if any) full-time officers and operate on lower per capita requirements. Because of the lower costs, they attract affiliates that are unwilling to pay the higher cost of per capita to the state body.

Since the AFL-CIO does not require affiliate basis with either central body—local or state—and since the local central body has monthly delegate meetings as compared with usually no more than one a year at the state level, it is natural and easy for some jurisdictions that belong to only one to try to use that body for its own expression of viewpoint.

The loosely defined structure and the open shop affiliate policy of the AFL-CIO puts both state and local central bodies at serious disadvantages in carrying out effective programs; sometimes this structure puts them in adversary positions.

New Discipline and Supervision for Central Bodies

The AFL-CIO, feeling that its national nonendorsement for the office of President in 1972 brought more divisiveness from its state central bodies than it had anticipated—more than it ever wants to see again—has embarked on a program of reorganizing its department of organization. However, the department is not being booked for Walter Reuther's "let's organize the unorganized under one banner" playbill. The department is going to deal primarily with AFL-CIO internal structure. It is going to try to see that AFL-CIO policy as enunciated by the leaders on the executive council is carried out consistently through the state and local central bodies.

President Meany looks on these local central bodies as appendages of the AFL-CIO. The fact that the financial support of these bodies does not come from either international unions or the AFL-CIO, but from the local unions that are willing to pay the open shop tax, will leave deep grievances if the new department is heavy-handed in meting out discipline. Local unions may just back out of continuing affiliation if their leaders and members begin to feel that only a small part of their central bodies belong to those paying the freight.

Limitations on State Leadership Potential

The quality of many state leaders impairs the effectiveness of the state bodies to carry on their public spokesmanship for "all of the AFL-CIO." For one thing, it is difficult to recruit top leadership, either from an employer's payroll or from local and international union payrolls, to run for short-term positions. Beyond this, most state positions are paid sparingly. True, they should not be paid luxuriously, but state executive officers generally make less than business managers of the larger local unions and considerably less than any international union pays its professional staff in the area. Since most executive officers are paid at annual median salaries of under $18,000 across the state bodies, it is difficult to hire knowledgeable and competent staff at commensurately lower figures. As a result, most states have no staff other than one or two office secretaries and one or two executive officers. The task of carrying the policies of the AFL-CIO, let alone the state AFL-CIO, to a great body of membership is thus accomplished with only fractional success.

In the process of failing to attract leaders who want to lead with honest candor, the tendency for many state leaders is to curry favor from the top levels of the AFL-CIO. Naturally, there are exceptions to this, but it is inevitable that leaders like to receive attention. In fact, goodwill from the leaders of any institution is sometimes more rewarding for a local officer than doing the job that ought to be done for the people who elected him in the first place. Many state and local central body leaders find themselves trapped by seeking the blessings that they feel can best be bestowed from on high.

Despite Roadblocks, Some States Do Well

In spite of all of this, there have been some exceptionally fine accomplishments at the state levels of the AFL-CIO because leaders were willing to push ahead—and in some instances, had sufficient resources to do so quite safely.

In the state of Washington, for instance, the limitation by successful ballot initiative on the rates of interest that financial institutions can place upon loans and installment buying came from the state AFL-CIO's program. In Arkansas, workmen's compensation was almost meaningless until a state ballot initiative came out of the Arkansas AFL-CIO and was adopted by the broad public support garnered from its sole effort. The state AFL-CIO bodies in Oklahoma and New Mexico have been remarkably effective in public relations and in their respective legislatures because of aggressive, competent leadership. Both states have union memberships that are proportionately a much smaller segment of the total work force than the national average, yet they have both withstood major efforts to impose the compulsory union shop and have assisted in upgrading both states' educational and public employee bargaining laws.

In Rhode Island, Connecticut, Massachusetts, Pennsylvania, and Michigan, the state central bodies were the keystones to the statutory gains for the right of public employees to be recognized and bargain collectively. In Texas, one of the best structured state AFL-CIO departmental programs in the nation has been put together—especially in youth and women's education and public relations aimed at a broad-based citizens' coalition at both the polling place and in the state capital lobbies.

In Alabama and Mississippi, the leadership of the respective state central bodies fought on the side of civil rights when white citizens' councils were trying to hold the line of bigotry and hate at the working class level, and they have helped turn the tide of battle. In West Virginia and Kentucky, the education programs set up through the initiative of the state central bodies have been the principal weapons of combat against poverty. In North Carolina, monthly kits from union leadership carry the full story of how to organize, how to integrate, how to educate, and what the issues are that working people must fight to win within the state and through its Congresspersons. No international union had really thought it possible to carry on such a program, and no international union could have accomplished as much on its own.

In Ohio, a multicolored, highly readable, issue-oriented monthly publication reaches almost 600,000 households—an antidote to the commercialism of much of the general media and a working person's publication that few business firms can match. In South Dakota, the program that is being communicated by written word, pictures, cassette tapes, and electronic media from the leadership of a membership-small state body may soon lead to the restoration of union shop privileges in that state.

In Colorado, the most extensive service of representing union member claimants in reviewing judgments of government concerning job injury and job layoff benefits has provided the largest per capita returns to individuals of any state in the nation. Additionally, its state central body has sponsored a widely viewed weekly TV program on the ABC channels and community television in the state and adjoining states. In an 11-year period, over 300 local union leaders have been seen and heard, over 1,200 community and national leaders have joined in conversation on "labor's language," and the AFL-CIO has had its public credibility enhanced.

Underfinanced, undermanned, oversupervised from above, the state central bodies have been unable to be as effective as union democracy would otherwise permit. New leadership in the AFL-CIO and its international unions might view these unique institutions within the labor structure with more trust in the future; if they do, these leaders must make certain that state central bodies are supported from the bottom up, not bossed from the top down. "Caught in the middle" is not a very effective posture for advancing any positive interest of the AFL-CIO.

AN EXAMPLE OF A STATE BODY

The Nixon reelection campaign of 1972 provided the AFL-CIO with its most severe leadership trauma since the merger convention of 1955. Part of the reason for creating the hyphenated union of the former American Federation of Labor and Congress of Industrial Organizations was the political clout that George Meany and Walter Reuther foresaw. But Reuther did not live to see Meany's disenchantment with the Democratic convention of 1972. If he had been alive, perhaps his strong voice might have reminded the leaders of the well-documented record in the case of the American workers versus Richard M. Nixon. Meany declared the race between Nixon and the Democrats to be a standoff. His "neutrality" proclamation startled grass-roots labor leadership.

"A Creature of the AFL-CIO"

One of the issues at the AFL-CIO's tenth constitutional (biennial) convention in October, 1972, was the Colorado Labor Council's case against a Meany trusteeship. The council had refused to back away from its endorsement of George McGovern as the only realistic way to defeat Richard Nixon.

The chronology of the reason for the council's appeal to the AFL-CIO's highest tribunal went something like this:

July 19, 1972—President Meany announced that "Under the circumstances the AFL-CIO will refrain from endorsing either candidate for President of the U.S. Affiliates, however, are free to do as they choose."

Between July 19 and August 7, when the Committee on Political Education (COPE) of Colorado voted unanimously to endorse Senator McGovern, the council had been advised verbally that Meany would instruct all state central bodies not to endorse. Meany's written notice that came a few days later said nothing about nonendorsement. It said that state bodies were to conform to policies of the AFL-CIO and its affiliated international and national unions.

Colorado's board stood with its COPE endorsement, 28-to-1, on August 17, 1972, even though Meany had ordered the council to rescind its endorsement four days earlier.

CLC's board defied Meany based on the following reasoning: (1) the constitution of the AFL-CIO declares a state central body to be an affiliate; (2) 58 of 59 resolutions of the AFL-CIO in the three and one-half years preceding the summer of '72 had concluded for one reason or another that the President should be "dumped." That was policy—AFL-CIO policy.

So CLC told Meany that it was an affiliate and that he did not have the right to order it to rescind its action or to place it under his trusteeship.

Support in Spite of Pressure

CLC received federal district court protection from trusteeship on October 2, 1972. The majority of Colorado AFL-CIO local unions continued to support their state council. The Tenth Circuit Court reversed the district court on June 20, 1973, and on July 9, Meany ordered Colorado local unions to cease financial payments to CLC.

In spite of these actions by the AFL-CIO president, almost half of the Colorado council's local affiliates continued to pay monthly per capita. These locals were, for the most part, defying the illegal orders of their parent unions.

But the pressures of an economic boycott "in house" were such that the board of the Colorado Labor Council voted reluctantly and under protest to end its independent stand against Meany on November 3, 1973. The ironies of that decision were self-evident: (1) what Colorado had said about the Nixon administration in August, 1972, was all too apparent in fact before midyear, 1973; (2) the great bulk of the rank-and-file membership and leadership in Colorado still supported the CLC stance but found their relationships with their respective international unions threatened; and (3) no state labor organization can perform adequate services for its affiliates if its income is drastically reduced and competent staff have to be laid off. On November 16, 1973, the trusteeship began under protest.

A Handpicked Review Committee

Inevitably, a five-member committee picked by President Meany to review the Colorado appeal from the trusteeship at the October, 1973, convention could conclude only one thing—that a state labor body cannot defy the AFL-CIO president.

Even the Tenth Circuit Court refused to concern itself about any bill of rights in federal law that might protect a state body. The court, looking shakily through the eyes of an *amicus curiae* brief from the Secretary of Labor in support of President Meany, concluded that probably a state labor body "is not a subordinate body." Under federal law, a subordinate body is a labor organization, and the CLC was not a labor organization. The circuit court went on to conclude that the district court in 1972 should never have entertained the presence of CLC in its courtroom. Although the Tenth Circuit Court expressed some doubt in its own decision, it admitted that it had to rule. It ordered the federal district court to dismiss its injunction against

Meany's trusteeshp of CLC and simultaneously denied Meany a legal order of trusteeship.

The effect of what it said was that no one other than Meany and the AFL-CIO could interpret the AFL-CIO constitution. A state labor body—in this case, CLC—is an "affiliate" in the constitution. Meany said: "I say, not so!"

The court also said that only Meany and the AFL-CIO governing body could determine what they meant when they said that AFL-CIO affiliates could do as they chose in the matter of an endorsement for the U.S. Presidency.

"You Shouldn't Have Looked"

Thus, the Tenth Circuit concluded that Colorado Federal District Court Judge Fred Winner had no business looking at what it found because it was not entitled to look at "hornbook law."

CLC appealed no further through the courts. It's a long wait at the doors of the Supreme Court of the United States. They did appeal to the AFL-CIO convention (a body that permits an open roll call vote where the larger international unions, whose presidents serve on President Meany's AFL-CIO executive council, could hardly reverse either Meany or its own top officers).

The statement that follows is CLC's last appeal—the convention floor statement in response to the committee's recommendation to sustain Meany's trusteeship. After the statement, the voice vote was so close that the chairman of the convention was unsure. But a roll call would have sustained George Meany—more than one year after his "neutrality for Nixon."

Appeal Statement of the Colorado Labor Council, AFL-CIO to the Tenth Constitutional Convention of the AFL-CIO

by Herrick S. Roth, President, CLC, AFL-CIO

This may be called a Colorado appeal; more than likely it is an appeal on behalf of many states and millions of AFL-CIO members who could buy neither neutrality nor playing dead when the White House and the prime leadership of our nation was at stake.

For all of us here, today, our principal stake is the security of our own union; our secondary stake is the growth and expansion of all unions—the labor movement; and neither stake is secure if America as a nation is beset by corruption by its own elected chief of state.

If we had not known that chief of state so well on July 19, 1972, the leadership of the AFL-CIO nearer its grass roots out across the countryside might not have reacted so unbelievingly when the White House was given a labor blessing of neutrality.

This is a Colorado appeal in the sense that it is not a one-man appeal. If a referendum of the 120,000 plus Colorado AFL-CIO members were demanded by this convention—and they are the members of our very same unions who are delegated to sit among us here today—we have confidence that the results would show you every evidence that the appeal is strongly supported. It was true on the dates of August 7 and August 17, 1972, when Colorado took its action. It is equally true now or we would not be here appealing anything.

A Lou Harris poll then and today would not only prove the case of how strong the majority of AFL-CIO membership is in Colorado on our side; it would make every delegate to this convention stop and take notice of what is really going on in the nation's workplaces.

We will not repeat here the written statements of appeal which we have made repeatedly since August 17, 1972; you have available to you the printed text of the abbreviated appeal put before the Appeals Committee of this convention. We repeat only that we are not corrupt; we are not mismanaged; we are in good stead with both members and the public-at-large; we were not the ones who violated either AFL-CIO practices and policy or the AFL-CIO constitution; and a trusteeship for the purposes stated is not legal, timely, or in the spirit of the good purposes of the AFL-CIO.

If you consider well what we have just stated, then none of us need ask why would the least among us persist in dogged determination to resist the directive of the top officer of the AFL-CIO, a House of Labor which has grown and stood tall when our workers and citizens have been worst oppressed.

Why was the unrest heightened in the union halls of the nation in 1972 and why does Colorado's one percent fraction of this our total AFL-CIO membership still insist that it be heard here, today, when obviously it is not even the tail to wag the dog—a limp tail on which it is only the knot at the end?

The more basic question confronting us in this convention hall, today, is just what is our proud labor movement all about in 1973? Do we know our course? If so, is it the course that we should be pursuing to serve the best interests of the work force of America? Failing in that positive pursuit, we fail the nation.

Colorado stood its ground in this, the AFL-CIO, in 1972, not because we found great comfort, generally speaking, in the candidate of our choice for the White House. We found in him an alternative; his candidacy was far superior to neutrality; and until this nation finds a better alternative of its own, there will be a White House and there will be an occupant.

All political choices are relative; sometimes the choices are more difficult to make; but neutrality is no choice in the American Republic because neutrality serves the status quo, deadens the spirit, destroys initiative, divides both loyal and committed alike, and thus makes mockery of the American system and its viability and its vitality, without which we would have no so-called free trade union movement.

Colorado stood its ground because it understood the difference between labor as a movement and labor at the bargaining table. If we profess to believe in political involvement and action, then it is well that we not forget that not all friends are always that friendly, but they are infinitely more friendly than an enemy. Any enemy is never friendly until converted, and all the evidence (1) of 1972 and before; (2) of 1972 even from July 19 through November 7; and (3) of the year since the convening of the second term of the top official in our land leads to the same undeniable conclusion: the man in the White House has not been converted and deserved, in the public interest, everything except the landslide needle of neutrality from some of the top leaders in our labor movement.

It is well that we believe who we say we are. If we do not believe, then we corrupt not only ourselves but we contribute to the deterioration of our nation's heritage and the undermining of the rights of our members in our union halls.

If we have forgotten who we say we are, return to New York's armory and the victory of December, 1955, and recall that this, our AFL-CIO, is an expression of the hopes and aspirations of the working people of America. Must we say to working people that they cannot in their own communities and states of this nation express who best satisfies those hopes and aspirations in the office of the Presidency just because others fail to do so?

If we have forgotten, it is best to repledge ourselves to "the more effective organization of working men and women; to the securing to them of full recognition and enjoyment of the rights to which they are justly entitled; to the achievement of ever higher standards of living and working conditions; to the attainment of security for all the people; to the enjoyment of the leisure which their skills make possible; and to the strengthening and extension of our way of life and the fundamental freedoms which are the basis of our democratic society."

If we do all this, do we reassure anyone in the workplace about any of these incontestable goals by permitting orders emanating from any single office anyplace in the structure of American trade unionism to be aimed at the destruction of the right to think and to assemble and to dissent and to propose and to activate—even if those orders come clothed in benevolent wisdom rather than unmistakable cunning?

We shall combat resolutely the forces which seek to undermine the democratic institutions of our nation and to enslave the human soul. This is our pledge—to win full respect for the dignity of the human individual whom our unions serve.

The 1972 July 19 statement of the AFL-CIO Executive Council—not Colorado or any other central body in this convention hall—initiated the action that was a blow to us all. It is the assertion of the Colorado Labor Council, AFL-CIO, that our actions of the past year more appropriately stand up to the judgment of what we say the AFL-CIO is than the actions of those whose orders have been placed upon us.

Now, the judgment of this convention will rule on that contention and our conviction. It is in your hands, for better or for worse.

One Year Earlier

The preceding statement is put in better perspective when we turn back one year, to the time I delivered a speech at the Colorado Labor Council convention. That convention followed by two days the favorable decision of the federal district court of Colorado that prevented for almost one year President Meany's trusteeship of the council. The speech follows.

We are gathered today because an issue of import to trade unionists in our land was tilted out of focus on a date that might, in labor history, be deemed significant—July 19, 1972.

A full head of steam was dissipated on that day. The valves were blown. The piston stroke weakened. The condensation of hot power aimed in the direction of challenging the competency and motivation of the President of this nation suddenly spewed directionless along the track bed. Evaporation misted the atmosphere; the drive wheels creaked to a halt; the full crew shook heads in disbelief; the power and seeming authority of positive direction were at a standstill on the mainline.

If, indeed, repairs were expected by the chief of the line and his cohorts, they were not forthcoming. In effect, from the well-outfitted interiors of the stalled mainliner, the official in charge extended remarks to certain branch line service that seemed to suggest it could not permit its rolling stock to move in a forward direction; backing up to go someplace was reluctantly allowed on the sidetracks.

It would have been much easier for the small segment of the American trade union trackage designated as Colorado to back up the grade. Like driving a tunnel through our own mightly mountains at the continental top of America, however, we mapped out forward motion, drove our course, were not impeded by artificial roadblocks, and have moved through the toughest of the mountainous barriers. We now look ahead to horizons beyond for better trackage and destinations worthy of the dignity of our union members "on board."

We are not here today to condemn the persons as persons who are mainline directors. We are here to see that reconstruction fits the purposes for which the system was established—that the directors are to serve the paying customers, without which there would be neither trunk nor feeder lines. The chief of the crew and the crew of the chief are paid to give direction, not directives—direction that befits the needs, the desires, and the legitimate requirements of the customers, who in turn provide the resources that make the system in operation worthy of its existence.

From figures of speech, we turn to the realism of this convention. This council has achieved its right to survive, serve, and lead. We are here today to put the focus on course—to ask what a "more perfect union," cast in the words of America's founders, really means. Domestic tranquility? Common defense? General welfare? Blessings of liberty? Insure—provide—promote—secure? These were their words.

In December, 1955, we pulled ourselves in the House of Labor so close together that only a hyphen separated us. The hyphen melted as the eyes of American trade unionism temporarily were lifted by "the establishment of this federation" —forming a more perfect union movement as "an expression of the hopes and aspirations of the working people of America."

Words are words and meaningless if only uttered. Ideals are worthy expressions, if those who state them are willing to find the pragmatic courses that reach out for the ideals rather than take the easy paths that bypass them.

The leaders in American labor, who today act as if the "objects and principles"—the ideals of American labor—are early sections of articles of constitutional pronouncement that never need to be looked back upon (once the leaders find comfort in those later articles that define how the same leaders are to be balloted into office by their own computation of numerical voting units which no other ballots can outnumber) are indeed short of sight, mind, and conscience. By so doing, they declare themselves not fit to lead and to serve the "workers (of America) without regard to race, creed, color, national origin, or ancestry" who are entitled to "share equally in the full benefits of union organization."

We are gathered here today to test, pragmatically, that charge not only to our leadership in this convention but to the leadership in the AFL-CIO across the land.

Since we last met in total convention on April 8 of this year, the board and committee on political education of this council have found thmselves testing the "fulfillment of these hopes and aspirations through the democratic processes within the framework of our constitutional government and consistent with our institutions and traditions."

We have in the interim come face to face on August 7, August 17, August 30, and September 28 and 29 with these challenges to "protect and strengthen our democratic institutions . . . to preserve and perpetuate the cherished traditions

of our democracy . . . to give constructive aid in promoting
the cause of peace and freedom in the world . . . to protect
the labor movement from any and all corrupt influences . . . to
safeguard the democratic character of the labor movement . . .
while preserving the independence of the labor movement
from political control."

Let us now put the matter of our gathering in direct
focus. Each of us here is now challenged to reject, modify,
and/or ratify the difficult but real steps that the leadership
of this council has taken since we last met.

Basic among the questions before you is the issue of the
corruption of power—the inhumanity of bigness. Bigness in
itself is not bad if its control is by the people by whom and
for whom it has been created and sanctioned. We in American
labor, as in American business and in American government,
must find the way of people involvement, either by new
forms and structures or by vitalization of existing organization
within the bigness that encompasses these very features.

What we proclaim here to ourselves is not just our
utter disrespect for a bureaucracy in labor, business, or government that permits handing down unilateral orders from a
single officer or office to command people to do the bidding
of the order. The involvement and the determination of the
people, themselves, must be the rule of the day, and the officer
and office should serve the decision of the people—that
people cannot have served upon them the order of an office
or officer.

Power that emanates from the program and the vote of
the people who are to be affected by the administration of
that power does not corrupt itself until the administrator
abuses the power. People who by apathy, indifference, or
fear refuse to end the abuse, even while they recognize it
for what it is, then delay the day of just decision.

There are some of our brothers and sisters who are
temporarily absent from us today; they are faltering under
the heavy pressure of unilateral rule within their respective
jurisdictions; they are seeking to regroup their own people
to make their own collective judgments in their own union
halls here at home in Colorado; they are summoning the
good sense and courage needed to fight the erroneous autocracy of a system that was once established to secure the
blessings of liberty; they will find those courses and be with

us again very shortly, we feel confident. We will welcome them back to the Colorado fold of labor that this council's actions continue to seek to secure.

There is in America's White House a man whose placid countenance oft betrays his revelling in the divisiveness that he has successfully thrust upon some of our labor leadership, whose actions show their willingness to sanction or even to promote the division in our ranks. History is replete with such game playing in the temples of power. In 1972, the bidding and the maneuvers of the chiefs among us, aimed within our land and between the lands of the world at weakening the power of decision of free peoples, is of exceedingly greater consequence than the moves on the boards of the new international sport of chess.

So we are here today because we have been favored by the judgments of two constitutional systems—the AFL-CIO and the United States of America. These systems have said to us, up to today, that the leadership of this council has tried to sense, report, and act upon what seems to be the consensus and direction of its own memberships. This convention can confirm, amend, or deny that assertion, for it is not meant as a self-proclamation.

In the more appropriate language of a "Texanism" that a trade union supporter in Colorado phoned into our office a few days ago, we are here today because "It's the way you show up at the showdown that counts."

Judicial Determinations by the Federal Court

As an appropriate conclusion to this part, there is reprinted on pp. 154–173 the full texts of the federal district court findings which maintained the integrity of the Colorado Labor Council, AFL-CIO, from October 2, 1972, until June 20, 1973; the Tenth Circuit United States Court of Appeals determination that the Colorado Labor Council, AFL-CIO, did not have standing in the district court, filed on June 20, 1973; and the petition of the Colorado Labor Council, AFL-CIO, for rehearsing before the circuit court, which denied the petition in August, 1973.

6

Bottom of the Heap

A local central body has even more liabilities than a state central body. It has a smaller potential of support. By the very existence of a state central body, it is preempted from having its per capita support be even as great as the state (the average per capita that states have been able to get their affiliates to tax themselves is less than 20¢ per month per member; the average for the local central bodies is half that amount).

Local central bodies are of all kinds: some cover city jurisdictions, some cover metropolitan areas, and some cover several counties. Some metropolitan areas have several local central bodies, bringing up the controversy of how many members of metro or statewide locals should be affiliated with each of the central bodies.

Some local bodies have delegate meetings more than once a month, and some have delegate meetings monthly. In either event, as is the case with local unions, unless there are some very exciting programs added to the agenda, they are usually poorly attended.

Over 700 Local Area AFL-CIO Bodies

There are over 700 local central bodies by the AFL-CIO. They deal directly with the national AFL-CIO, not in conjunction with or through the state organizations. Local central bodies may affiliate themselves for convention delegate purposes with the state group; other relationships between the state and local bodies depend upon the cooperative initiatives and leadership of the respective officers.

Of the 700, only slightly more than 100 have a full-time officer or office (with a part-time or full-time secretary and office services). Usually, these are larger city central bodies.

The local central bodies of the AFL-CIO have an affiliate membership of less than 50 percent of the available AFL-CIO member-ship across the country. About 5 percent of that membership is com-pletely outside the geographical limits of the local central bodies. But the remaining 45 percent nonmembership attests to a weakness that even the state "open shop" memberships do not face.

Some Unusual Local Central Bodies

There are some unusual local central bodies in the nation. Some are staffed and some are not.

If every local central body published a widely circulated news-letter that is as readable and as to the point as that published by the top-flight Greater Cincinnati AFL-CIO, local issues would not go unnoticed in the local union halls. The Los Angeles County Federation of Labor (LACFL) is staffed for service as if it were a large local union or a sophisticated state central body. Its newspaper, the *Los Angeles Citizen,* is one of the liveliest news organs available in either the public or in-house media. The LACFL is more than half again as large as the California Labor Federation, the state body.

In fact, if it were not for Los Angeles, New York City, Detroit, and Chicago among the large city federations, the local area and city central bodies would come up with an even smaller percentage of AFL-CIO membership across the nation.

Chicago operates its own radio station, which provides public service programs as well as making a profit. Detroit has one of the most active minority-related programs across the country. The New York Central Labor Council operates an educational program that provides extension classes on hundreds of subjects from community vocational to university levels.

The local central bodies, if structured and funded properly, could address themselves very effectively in all of the large and small cities of the nation to the problems of urban government and living.

One Hundred Percent Affiliation Needed

In even the least well organized cities of the country, a one hundred percent affiliated and fully funded local central body could be a most effective force. School systems could get direct attention—in terms of program, facilities, curriculum, teaching, continuing edu-cation, work-study schooling, equal-opportunity and equal-quality education for all students, equitable bases of tax support—to name some areas almost totally ignored by the present inadequate local central bodies.

There are many other issues that could be dealt with more effectively. Governmental reorganization could be put in total focus so that urban government could replace the inefficient, overlapping multiplicity of government subdivisions that crisscross metro areas. Urban renewal could be expanded from core city to suburb; parks and recreation could be brought close to high-rise population areas; rapid transit could alleviate the congestion on city streets; community education centers, libraries, and museums could be made equally available to total metro areas; police, fire, sanitation, and utility services could be provided uniformly to the total urban area.

Future urban growth could be planned to bring jobs closer to living areas; to make air and water less contaminated; to make health services available to all persons; to rehabilitate lawbreakers who are not criminally incompetent instead of incarcerating them to be dehumanized; to achieve security for all unions against the importation of strikebreakers into urban areas—these and other potential priorities could be addressed by effective AFL-CIO local central bodies.

Revision of structure and freeing the local memberships for involvement in local central body activities would give labor one of its most vital boosts. Then there would be no "bottom of the heap."

7

The Independents

How independent is independent?

In this case, I am speaking of the union that is not an affiliate of the AFL-CIO or its successor in future generations.

I am really speaking of the nonaffiliated.

The Nonaffiliated

The Teamsters and the UAW were the two largest nonaffiliates in 1974. They have already come in for enough discussion. They may in fact properly be better off outside the AFL-CIO than in it. But I must constantly assume that all of labor would be better off in one house that had some authority to do some general things on behalf of all workers that are better performed together than separately.

This chapter focuses on one union that was independent and nonaffiliated in 1974—the United Mine Workers. It is a case study in rejuvenation that provides hope for all of the labor movement. It may not be nonaffiliated for long—it may be the new base, as it once was the prime base, for putting labor's house together in new and productive fashion.

UNITED MINE WORKERS

The three new executive officers of UMWA declared 1973 "The Year of the Rank and File."

They had just concluded one year as the new leaders of the 84-year-old union. Selected by the rank and file from the rank and file, they had campaigned to reform the strife-torn union that had seen Joseph "Jock" Yablonski, murdered when he had sought to be the reform president of UMWA less than four years earlier. Jock had said upon announcing his candidacy in 1969, "It's time someone speaks up, no matter what the sacrifice may be." He and members of his family were the sacrifice, "slaughtered as the end result of a calculated contract murder plot involving many people," in the words of the UMW *Journal* of May 1, 1973.

What happened subsequent to the Yablonski tragedy was a re-determined effort by the rank and file to bring all persons responsible for the murders to trial and to conduct a secret-ballot election for the three top officers of the union under a polling booth supervision free of violence and intimidation.

Not all of those who planned and plotted the murder had a determination of their guilt or innocence made much before the end of 1974, but the nationwide UMWA election was completed in 1972, supervised by the federal government.

Battle for the Honest Ballot

The UMWA's constitutional provisions for the secret-ballot referendum of the membership for the election of officers were not necessarily followed to the letter in the latter years of John L. Lewis's presidency or during the term of his successor, Tony Boyle. In the Yablonski–Boyle elections, there was violence, ballot stealing, and ballot box stuffing, along with the murders. Boyle was certified as the plurality winner of that contest, but the rank-and-filers protested and sought relief to hold another election.

Landrum-Griffin's provisions had been limited by compromises at the time of passage to the use of the secret ballot (and the right of the government to supervise an election) only at the local union level. Thus, the law provided no ready relief in court to the petitioning rank and file. However, the commitment of the petitioners, the legal wisdom and perseverance of both Joseph L. Rauh, Jr., and Joseph (Chip) Yablonski, Jr., and the presentation of the facts of corruption and illegal ballot counting to both federal agencies and the court brought another election, which Boyle and his colleagues lost. The new officers appointed Chip Yablonski general counsel of the union.

In December, 1973, the forty-sixth constitutional convention of UMWA in Pittsburgh was presided over by a rank-and-filer who had never been to a convention previously. President Arnold Miller is a miner from West Virginia. He hadn't professed to be a presidential type when the rank-and-filers selected him. His colleagues had also made no pretensions of knowing all about the duties of a vice-president or of a secretary-treasurer. But when Miller, Mike Trbovich, and Harry Patrick showed up at the confluence of the Monongahela and the Allegheny rivers, they offered no apologies for their first year in office.

The Untrained Learned Their Jobs

All three made no bones about the fact that they had been elected to reform the union and to make it responsive to rank-and-file needs. Since they had to learn their jobs, they devoted more than ordinary efforts to the union.

Miller visited every one of the 22 districts in UMWA, where 140,000 miners in the union mine four out of five tons of American coal production. He went underground in mines in Nova Scotia, Appalachia, the Midwest, and the West where no union officer had set foot even above ground in years. And he met face to face with the large lingering minority of Tony Boyle supporters.

He avoided meeting members where it appeared his life might be in danger; otherwise, he talked and met and worked with the men of all ages who mine the coal—and it was obvious to them that he was one of them and had much to share with them, including his reasoned judgment.

When he appeared on radio and TV programs, his preshow nervousness was never more than the butterflies that the pros get before the game—he was impressive, not with his grammar, but with his commitment, his common sense, and his clarity of language. There was never any trouble knowing what he was saying or how he meant it. He came through.

Arnold Miller must have had some understanding about the wide world about him even though he had buried his work life under the mountains of West Virginia for several score of years. In addition to meeting the media, he was willing to put down his thoughts on the energy crisis in the fall of 1973 for the articulate, "looking to the future" membership of Robert Maynard Hutchins's Center for the Study of Democratic Institutions.

He has not apologized for his views as only a coal miner. He has responded to requests to state the position of UMWA as if the persons who sought his views were not trying to trip him up because he had not been there before but meant to have his views for what they were worth. They have been worth it. I have every confidence they will continue to be.

Where Miller has not traveled, Trbovich and Patrick have. Together they have revamped and staffed a safety division in UMWA that will keep members aware of their legal and personal rights to work and to live safely while mining coal. Knowledgeable rank-and-filers have been brought into the division. The staffers filed more claims in their first year than had been filed in the previous decade against unsafe mine operations and in support of miners who were suspended or fired because they refused to operate unsafe equipment. The UMWA officers and the safety division under Trbovich's special direction have used the provisions of the 1972 amendments to the Coal Mine Health & Safety Act to secure enforcement, upgrade state laws to at least federal levels, and to make certain that the new Mining Enforcement and Safety Administration (MESA) avoids the conflicts of interest that the Bureau of Mines used to face in its former dual task of developing mineral resources and enforcing mine safety.

Effective, Dramatic Fiscal Measures

Patrick has been equally effective. It didn't take time for him to learn the books, even though he had never pushed a treasurer's pencil before. He helped dispose of the luxury trappings of the predecessor officers and staff—the Cadillacs, the corporate-executive-style salaries, the unlimited expense accounts. In one year, he trimmed over half a million dollars from salaries and expenses, yet officers and staff are still paid well and "go wherever business demands that they go without restriction." They just don't waste anymore.

He also looked over very carefully the underfunded and separately administered UMWA Welfare Fund in terms of its financial needs and proposed a fiscally sound recommendation for the 1974 industry contract. He assessed and made recommendations regarding the extensive real estate holdings of UMWA in downtown Washington, D.C. His report showed more than just addition and subtraction; he analyzed the substance of the programs, properties, revenues, and costs that relate to the operation he has established.

The officers have brought to headquarters a new kind of staff that in many instances has administrative knowledge and training that none of the three officers possessed. These professionals find their new positions exciting because of the determination and judgment that the officers have exhibited.

Some of the miners who met the staff for the first time in December, 1973, at Pittsburgh, may have been taken a little aback by their youth and hair styles. Not all of the new staff members have been miners. They are hard-working, visionary people, some of whom have had as their background Vista or Peace Corps service. They may not have looked as if they would be at home with the rank-and-filer officers, but they were found to be.

Although negotiations and UMWA national bargaining council actions both reportedly approached the brink of failure, President Arnold Miller and his fellow officers and staff did not fail in 1974. If old-line Tony Boyle supporters—coincidentally aided by some local leaders who found new political opportunities in the union's new open democracy—thought Miller-Trbovich-Patrick could be cut down by the rank and file, they were wrong. UMWA concluded its most comprehensive national agreement in 1974. The members were not misled.

The United Mine Workers *Journal* still appears in a magazine style newsprint, but its twice-monthly publication has been filled with the same new spirit of democracy that even the "opposition" delegates seemed to feel before the 1973 convention had passed.

The rank-and-file members are being interviewed in all UMWA districts on every conceivable subject that concerns the miner's daily work life—even on the subject of whether or not women ought to work in the mines.

The extensive comment on shift rotation early in 1973 developed a stream of union responses in the expanding letters-to-the editor pages that make it quite clear that shift rotation contributes to mine safety when the men who work the shifts make their own determination as to how shifts are assigned. If applied in new contracts, it could throw seniority bidding out the window in some mines and reinstate it in others, but at least the UMWA officers know where the decision ought to be made.

The organizing drive already under way is unlike any that UMWA has seen in years. There are more nonunion than union operations in several sections of the country—eastern Kentucky and Tennessee, the Northwest, and the Mountain states—especially the new strip-mining areas. Since the greatest area of unmined low-sulphur coal in the world may become the energy replacement source for oil by 1985, UMWA is looking to the strips of the central and upper Mountain and Plains states as well as to the valleys of central Appalachia.

Through the *Journal* and other communications, including perhaps the best graphic historical display assembled by any union for its convention, UMWA is refreshing members' minds on both the history of the struggles in the coalfields and who the operators have been and are.

Organizing in Nonunion Territory

It reinforces UMWA's leadership recommendations that non-union Duke Power country, including Harlan County, Kentucky, where violence and the great strike of 1931 crunched the union, can and must be organized.

The young Brookside strikers came to the convention, representing the cost and the need of organization in the coalfields where output will be doubling in the 1970s. Florence Reese, aging but still vital and in good voice, sang her original great UMWA hymn that she "accidentally composed way back when"—"Which Side Are You on, Boys?"

This is Arnold Miller's, Mike Trbovich's, and Harry Patrick's query to the rank-and-filers throughout American labor. The query is being heard as it has not been heard for a half-century in UMWA. The roots of the Ludlow Massacre of April, 1914, and the Rockefellers' absentee ownership of the early 1900s will be reviewed in terms of the oil and copper industries' ownership of the great undeveloped coalfields of New Mexico, Colorado, Wyoming, Montana, and the Dakotas. Organizing teams will be moving in those areas, too —far removed geographically from Appalachia but not far removed from the new democracy of UMWA.

Using the Secret Ballot

Elections by secret ballot began in 1973 to replace the appointed holders of office on the executive board of UMWA and the presidents of the UMWA districts.

Miller and colleagues have proposed consolidation of some small districts for effective governing and more efficient use of revenues, but there has been some resistance.

Some, including very competent and sensitive staff members of the Welfare (Health) and Retirement Fund, have been concerned that the new officers will try to shape new policy for the otherwise independent fund. I would guess that if any new policies are shaped, they will not be aimed at the independent professional judgments that can now be exercised within the fund. Rather, there might be questions about whether or not certain areas of the fund's bureaucracy are serving the members—active and retired. We shall see!

Welfare No. 1 Bargaining Issue

Additionally, UMWA made sick pay and the amount of tonnage royalty supporting the Welfare and Retirement Fund the number one priorities on the 1974 bargaining table. With the achievement of these goals, there is no doubt that the fund's administration will be questioned only if the increased revenues are not properly allocated in terms of the needs and guarantees made to the membership and retirees.

Miller has pointed out on several occasions that most of the operators seemed to be supportive of the Boyle reelection effort. Fortunately, they have subsequently recognized that Boyle is through, the union had spoken through an honest ballot box, and that their own best interests would be served by getting the issues thrashed out on the bargaining table. Miller notes that bargaining will be tough—there are too many unmet needs of recent years that will have to go to the bargaining table. Additionally, the operators see that there are no ways to make deals from this point on. Bargaining is going to be for real. That's tough bargaining.

Arnold Miller calls on history in refreshing members' understanding of other days of "honest bargaining"—when UMWA's fifth president, John Mitchell, a firm yet honorable man, kept the faith of the miners as he stood his ground against the inflexible financial barons at the turn of the century in the anthracite fields.

John Pierpont Morgan and his "puppet operators," as the Hearst publications referred to them, thought they could get Mitchell and UMWA to accept a miserly settlement. The bargaining was tough and frustrating, but the rank and file stood with their chosen leader and won.

A New Breath from and by the Rank and File

In UMWA, there is a new breath of courage, a renewal in the belief that a worker can be selected by the ranks out of the ranks and be a good leader.

Patrick may be a desk officer instead of a bucket miner in 1974, but no one had to teach him what is significant, including this judgment: "Too many unions think in narrow terms. Our power is standing together as working people."

Mike Trbovich sees "organizing the unorganized workers . . . more than ever before, a prime requirement for this organization . . . and of all working people and [their] families." He underscores this by quoting the changes in the Supreme Court philosophy near the end of the late Charles Evans Hughes's term as Chief Justice: for the worker who "was nevertheless unable to leave the employer and resist arbitrary and unfair treatment . . . that union was essential to give laborers opportunity to deal on equality with their employer."

Patronizing Profits or People

Miller has staffed up the headquarters and field services of UMWA so that the facts will be known and will be laid clearly on the bargaining table. He makes it clear that he understands two basic things about coal: (1) a coal miner's job, even if made as safe as possible, will continue to be hard, dirty, tough work; and (2) coal as a resource will be kicked around politically if the government in Washington patronizes profits in preference to people.

He knows that coal can be mined ecologically *and* profitably. He knows that coal is not in short supply. In fact, petro coal of the West is available in ten times the quantity of all known U.S. oil reserves, liquid and shale, and even if American consumption per person tripled in the next century, coal could supply all the necessary pipeline gas and synthetic gasoline.

Small "d" Democratic Institutions

Arnold Miller also knows that democratic institutions are really not that well understood by even the public officeholders. Since politics and coal and profits are all bound together—nothing can be completely separated from its related parts, Miller notes—public officeholders had best learn quickly that a democratic institution can be "democratic."

He is in the process of evaluating just how difficult it is to understand and use democracy, but he knows it means involving people. That's why criticisms of his own regime are printed in the United Mine Workers *Journal* without any editing.

Democracy is of no value in any institution, including a union, if it doesn't work both ways, he contends. You don't criticize just to be criticizing, either, but it's easy eventually to separate criticism that is valid from criticism that is for the benefit of the person leveling it.

These latter points were borne out in 1973 for Miller when UMWA's detailed description of the arbitrary and inadequate work of safety administrator Donald Schlick in the Bureau of Mines finally brought the Nixon administration to deny him the top spot in MESA

—a spot he otherwise would have inherited. At first, administration spokesmen labeled the UMWA charges as typical labor propaganda; on second thought, with a review of the record, UMWA was vindicated as having a valid case against Schlick's operation. He was placed elsewhere.

Political Action and Impeachment

The UMWA 1973 convention turned to its new need to be involved in political action in every state where it had members and further adopted a position that the process of impeachment was made a part of government for good purpose. The reaction to UMWA's position was quite different from the reaction to the AFL-CIO's 1973–1974 drive to impeach Nixon.

In the UMWA's case, Miller-Trbovich-Patrick leveled tough charges at Richard Nixon but always related them to the welfare of working people. They never switched sides on the Nixon issue; they leveled the charges on a timely and factual basis. By contrast, President Meany and his AFL-CIO executive council went through the cycle with Nixon: we're against; we're neutral for; we're against. The latter 1974 stance was detailed as if the middle stance had never existed. UMWA, the outside public, and the Nixon administration all noted the difference and the inconsistency.

No Second-Guessing Members

The UMWA's new administrative officers feel that they are never going to second-guess the members. They will try to persuade the members, they say. They intend to admit their mistakes; where they cannot move as fast as they have promised change, they will state why as they still seek change. They will state what the positions of members are as soon as it is clear that these are the positions. This, they contend, will maintain their UMWA administration as "the years of the rank and file."

Inspiration of the Past for Present Use

At the Pittsburgh convention, Miller closed his report with a statement he felt represented what he believes. His research department had been digging into past, present, and future. It came from the past—from the forerunner of the UMWA, when the American Miners Association assembled to organize in Illinois in 1860.

The words bespeak the inspiration of the spirit of the Pittsburgh

1973 convention and Arnold Miller's low-key, common-sense, common-man leadership:

"Union is the great fundamental principle by which every object of importance is to be accomplished. Man is a social being and if left to himself, in an isolated condition, would be one of the weakest creatures; but associated with his kind he works wonders. Men can do jointly what they cannot do singly; and in the union of minds and hands, the concentration of their power becomes almost omnipotent.

"Nor is this all. Men not only accumulate power by union, but gain warmth and earnestness. There is an electric sympathy kindled, and the attractive forces inherent in human nature are called into action; and a stream of generous emotion, of a friendly regard for each other, binds together and animates the whole."

Miller continued with his own words: "We are bound together still, sometimes more than we realize. We are a union of coal miners —one and indissoluble—and proud of it."

He and his colleagues have returned UMWA to the rank and file; an almost impossible task, they often thought, but they have persisted and are succeeding.

At the Pittsburgh convention, he invited to the podium the representatives of activist unionism, people from such key unions as the Machinists, Steelworkers, AFSCME, Clothing Workers, OCAW, and UAW. There were also several AFL-CIO state leaders, Canadian and British labor leaders, political leaders of both Canada and the U.S., and rank-and-filers and ethnic minorities who are contributing to new democratic trends in American labor. These guests suggest the rank-and-file leadership want not just a union but a movement.

Additionally, extensive floor and committee debate on over 70 issues of direct interest to either miners or any other trade unionists made the give and take of the convention a living example of what Arnold Miller hopes will catch on: every worker is entitled to be involved, to be heard, and to participate in the key decisions. He is also entitled to get the facts so that he can make intelligent choices.

UMWA is not afraid of the raw democracy that comes when every member participates in building the union decision.

8

Labor and Government

Labor has a special identification with government in several ways. For one thing, labor has been a department of the federal government for over 60 years.

Occasionally, it is proposed that government be reorganized, "streamlined." When that is proposed, labor is usually on the reorganization chart as a part of another department. However, the final decision is normally not to streamline but to add. The Labor Department will probably be with us for another generation or two, if not for the life of the nation.

Labor would not be a viable part of the government if it were not for trade unions. Yet, as a department, it is intended to provide services and regulations for every facet of the world of work—the business side, the governmental side (in part), the nonunion workers' side, as well as the union workers' side.

Labor's Pursuit of Abuse Put Labor in Government

There would be few divisions or agencies related to the Department of Labor if there had been no laws concerning child labor, health and safety, equal employment opportunity, job training, mediation and conciliation, apprenticeship and training, minimum wages, fair labor standards, union structure, and other work-related areas. Most of these laws would never have been put on the books if it had not been for workers themselves seeking correction of abuses of persons in the workplace.

Workers have not set up ad hoc committees to deal with each of these issues as they arose. They have spoken up to government through their labor organizations. The Department of Labor was one of the indirect creations of this united voice known as the trade union movement.

Some states have labor departments also. Some states have divisions within other departments that are burdened with such descriptions as "industrial relations" or "commerce and industry." But labor is very much in the official halls of government, even when it is not one of the principal executive departments of state and local governments.

Labor as Lobbyist

Another of labor's identifications with government is in its role as a citizens' or people's lobby.

During my own time of representing organized working people in the lobbies of my own state's legislative body, I wore the identification badge the rules require but added to it the description, "The People's Lobby." Some persons would dispute that claim, but the fact is that most AFL-CIO lobbyists at every level of government are lobbying more often on general citizen issues than on specific trade union proposals.

Labor is a public voice for consumer interests, for educational needs, for governmental reorganization, for legislative reforms, for equal rights, for urban renewal, and for many other community and individual benefits that provide better living under law. This is a special identification with government.

Labor at the Ballot Box

Labor also identifies with government by taking positions on ballot choices, both candidates and issues.

Sam Gompers' dictum has become the byword of all trade unions, but particularly those in the AFL-CIO and the independent blue-collar trades: "Elect your friends and defeat your enemies."

Union leaders relate to Gompers' expression quite readily. They generally understand that people can win if they unite in supporting candidates sympathetic to working people as contrasted with those favoring special economic interests. Sound legislative or constitutional reform by ballot initiatives needs united support in the same manner.

A union is a grouping of people who, ostensibly, have certain goals in common. That being the case, all trade unions have established political-education and action programs. The best known of these programs is the AFL-CIO's Committee on Political Education (COPE).

Usually, labor's political efforts to elect friends and defeat enemies of working persons comprise one of the key relationships that labor has with government. That means that AFL-CIO COPE is the arm of a total House of Labor, full of trade unions aimed at reelecting friendly officeholders or seeking to replace unfriendly ones. If successful at the polls, labor makes its impact by its elected friends voting for significant legislation. This is labor's relationship at local, state, and federal levels.

Parallels to COPE

Some unions within the AFL-CIO operate within the framework of COPE, at least by coincidence, but prefer their own trademark on their political efforts.

The Machinists (IAM) has one of the oldest of the political traditions. They seek to promote one mind and purpose about political decisions across the membership of the union. To prove that these efforts are not partisan, IAM called its political committee the Machinists Non Partisan Political League (MNPPL).

Other parallels to COPE include ABC (Active Ballot Club) of the Retail Clerks and PEOPLE (AFSCME).

The PEOPLE program is President Jerry Wurf's and Secretary-Treasurer William Lucy's special push in nonfederal public employment. They believe that public employees are never going to be first class in the workplace until they are politically effective; that all public employees are on jobs that serve people; and that the right people in public office make it possible for the public employee to better serve all the people for whom government is created.

UAW has its Citizenship Program. UMWA has its new COMPAC (Coal Miners Political Action Committee). The Teamsters have DRIVE.

All of these programs aim to influence government in two basic ways: (1) direct support of favorable candidates for public office; (2) education, registration, and get-out-the-vote programs aimed at the trade unionist and his family.

Support to Labor's Friends

The direct support is both financial and nonfinancial. Most states do not have laws restricting political contributions by organizations, persons, or business. Certainly, one of the aftermaths of the Watergate disclosures, together with the "sunshine" open-disclosure laws enacted in Florida and adopted on the 1972 ballot in Colorado, will bring rapid change in campaign finance laws across the country at all levels of government.

But as of 1975 trade unions in most places can still legally vote contributions directly to candidates for nonfederal office. However, the record indicates that this kind of support is not given by many local unions or state or local labor bodies.

At the federal level, the Corrupt Practices Act and the 1974 Federal Campaign Practices Act clearly state that union treasury funds shall not be appropriated to candidates for federal office or to political parties that run candidates for federal office. The trade union answer to this relationship it has with several new state laws, including those in Hawaii, Washington, and California, places campaign-contribution restrictions on political committees, including union committees like COPE: More are in the offing. The federal government requires COPE, DRIVE, MNPPL, COMPAC, ABC, and similar groups to collect voluntary funds from union members on a person-to-person basis at a prescribed minimum cost. For instance, the COPE voluntary dollar program was conducted from 1956 through 1970 by asking state bodies and later national and international unions to have their local unions distribute COPE books of ten one-dollar tickets. Each union officer and steward was asked to sell ten union members one ticket each. Optional, little-used books had $5 and $10 tickets in Presidential years like 1964 and 1968.

In 1972, the $1 ticket ceased to be; a new book had 10 tickets at $2 each. That book was well circulated through AFL-CIO affiliate union halls until the July 19, 1972, proclamation of the executive council to be "neutral" in the Presidential race. The drop-off in pushing the COPE tickets after that was major throughout the country. COPE had difficulty making its quotas to grant at least $2,000 to each candidate for the Congress endorsed as "favorable and friendly" to organized labor.

Even at best, AFL-CIO COPE has done well to reach one member in seven for even $1 contributions in off-year elections. It has not done substantially better in Presidential years.

Most unions carefully account for every dollar of volunteer ticket purchases. They account by name. Probably this necessity hinders the contribution effort as much as anything. Everyone who handles the 10-ticket book must turn in through his local union both the unsold tickets (numbered serially) and the coupon attached to the tickets that have been sold (with the name, union identification, and personal address of each contributor on the coupon). These must be consolidated and sent to the union's national office. Finally, each union is asked to pass on 50 percent of these volunteer dollars to AFL-CIO COPE. Under law, COPE's certification is publicly re-ported. Behind each report at national union headquarters are the names and addresses covering every dollar contributed.

For this and other reasons, including their own separate efforts, almost one-fourth of the members of the AFL-CIO belong to unions that do not support the COPE effort.

Education, Register, Get out the Vote

In the educational effort, the registration drives, and the get-out-the-vote effort, AFL-CIO COPE retains a closer relationship of the trade union family to its governments—local, state, and national.

For its operating support of these programs in most states (in some states, there is little or no contribution), COPE assesses each union a percentage of the general per capita funds paid annually by that union. Payment is not compulsory, but the money that is received is carefully accounted for. It is sent to state central bodies only in return for receipts that make that party liable if the funds are spent on any campaign for federal office.

These funds provide literature, make possible the printing of voting records of incumbents and the pledges of the other candidates, and pay for baby-sitting while the women of the auxiliaries and the unions do the work of precincting members, assisting in getting them registered, and helping to get them to the polls on election day.

Trade Unionists and the Democratic Party

One of the problems of trade union electoral efforts relates to the identification of members' political persuasions. It was heavily Democratic in the New Deal days, blew cold for Harry Truman until his veto of Taft-Hartley in 1947, and came to the fore in 1964 when Barry Goldwater was the Republican candidate for President. He was known as Mr. Compulsory Open Shop. The labor identification with the Democratic party related more to the candidates for the Presidency in 1948 and 1964. Party identification was strong in the New Deal days because FDR and Congress put together a program that gave working people the hope of employment and family security.

The fact that this political party identification has not necessarily been strong so far in the 1970s may be explained by George Meany's reasons why he, personally, did not support either Nixon or McGovern in 1972. His assertion left large segments of the union population in political disarray. He said to the trade union Democrat that McGovern's 94 percent favorable COPE voting record in Congress was meaningless. Destruction of COPE's policy of supporting friends and defeating enemies at the level of the Presidency was a more damaging blow to labor's position at the polling place than Meany's obvious disenchantment with McGovern's Democratic nomination.

COPE's Temporary Trauma

When in late 1973 and early 1974 the AFL-CIO launched an impeach-Nixon drive, the headquarters released a thoroughly documented statement on Watergate. COPE stressed that impeachment was in the interests of restoring the American people's confidence in their government. Many union people reacted to COPE's effort to return to the rulebook by standing aside in disbelief, even though their political inclinations were anything but supportive of Mr. Nixon. Much union hall wrath has been directed at whether COPE's position was any more credible than that of the White House.

COPE survived these years of trauma because union people relate to their citizenship responsibilities and to support friends for election.

Unionization Within Government

Labor has another significant relationship to government in that unions organizing government employees have shown more membership growth in the period 1960–1974 than any sector of the union movement.

The fears of the doubters in other segments of the public are expressed by more than the right-to-work focus across the nation. There has now been established a parallel national group, seeking widespread financial support to be certain that the "worst fears of our people" are not to be realized by unions taking over government.

This Virginia-based national appeal, Americans Against Union Control of Government, is stressing as the "worst fears" that "big labor" will take over all government if "we, the people" do not guard against all unionization within the bureaucracies of American government.

Jerry Wurf, Albert Shanker, Jim Rademacher (NALC—letter carriers), Clyde Weber (AFGE—Government employees), Bill McClennan (IAFF—firefighters), and their colleagues are probably laughing in disbelief.

First of all, each of them knows how difficult it is to organize any union, let alone one of public employees. Next, they know how nearly impossible it is to fashion and pass legislation that even defines a reasonable procedure for government workers to seek the collective bargaining right and sign a contract covering only a small part of their working conditions. Neither the general public nor the liberal legislators in Washington, D.C., or any state capitol are easily persuaded to legislate well for either the public worker's or the farm worker's interest.

Lastly, the AFL-CIO itself, even with support resolutions on the books, has given no special priority to lobbying in Congress for even a partial national labor law for public employees.

In states like Hawaii, Wisconsin, Michigan, and Pennsylvania, where public employee bargaining laws are in effect that cover either all or large segments of state and local government employment, the state AFL-CIO central bodies aided the public employee unions to get or extend laws; but even the private-sector trade unionists see these "best" of laws as incomplete.

State Public Employee Bargaining Laws Slow to Come

Current assessment of laws like those in Pennsylvania and Wisconsin is that the laws are working and that public service has improved through the operation of the laws, even though there have been some strikes (especially by teachers). The public officials who are elected and the public officials who administer these laws find that the bargained contract has reduced work force turnover and generally upgraded service efficiency as wages and working conditions have been been improved by union agreements.

These are, at best, preliminary evaluations.

I simply must comment, having been a public employee myself prior to the recognition of any bargaining right for such employees, that the last thing any American should feel is that unions will take over government through the organization of the workers in the public sectors. Even if all of this work force—almost one in five of all nonmilitary and nonfarm employment in America—were organized, it would be in competing jurisdictions. More than that, these workers are taxpayers, too, and are everyone's fifth neighbor down the street. Their daily task is to make government a better service organization for themselves as well as the other 80 percent of Americans.

Fear not.

Unions have a very direct interest in government—federal, state, and local—but unions are made up of citizens, too. They never see their role as that of running government or private business.

At best, unions should improve government by the daily work their members perform. At worst, unions will have difficulty organizing the larger numbers of government workers. Unless organized, workers cannot be responsible for sharing with government managers (bureaucrats, in the best sense) a "better way to serve the public."

9

Trade Union Democracy

This book has been continually dealing with trade union democracy.

In this chapter, we merely explore in particular the shortcomings and strengths of what American trade union domocracy is.

It is diversified, and in that respect, has strength. There is no common system that is imposed, as it is argued is the case in the totalitarian nations.

A major shortcoming is that it does little training for involvement and leadership of members. It is beset with the further shortcoming that the American system of public education makes little reference either by activity or academic pursuit to trade union halls.

Schools Deficient in Training for Democracy

Additionally, American schools do not promote a participatory understanding of the republican democracy that America is. In other words, there is little direct effort to make even the secondary student feel the responsibility of representative government within his school situation. At best, there is still a superficial attest to student government as relating to an understanding of the real-life local, state, and federal government (the federalism of our republican democracy).

Unions in America suffer because the trade union hall is based upon representative or republican democracy. If members have not had prior training as to how and why democracy works, then trade union democracy suffers. This is the reason why most of Chapter 7 was devoted to describing what the UMWA is doing under its new union leadership to strengthen participatory democracy within a union. I believe that this will not be a short-lived event.

The union will have its problems and trauma along the road. The most difficult system to administer well is a system of governing that invites everyone to participate—Come on in, the water's fine. The calmness of the pool is disturbed by the waves of the people who are splashing around, trying to find the direction to swim.

Making Gains but Losing Soul

There is strong evidence that a number of unions that were founded with democratic intent have achieved gains in the bargained contract but have lost the soul of trade union democracy over the years.

Is there any scheme or principle or fair ethical practice that warrants a salary higher than $50,000 for any top leader in any union position in this nation? If trade union democracy had been fully participatory since the Wagner Act's passage, there would be no job priced higher than that. Yet, there are union jobs priced higher than that, and they in no way relate to what the worker whose dues supports these jobs makes or expects of his leaders.

This is not a criticism of the trade union movement, as such. It is the inevitable result of both members and leaders not understanding what it means to secure and administer a representative democracy in their own unions.

Some unions have slipped back from democratic processes after merger. In the process, in order to grow larger, be less competitive, and ostensibly serve members better, the union that had the secret ballot might have had to give it up as a condition of merger with the union that did not use the secret ballot. Once this sacrifice is made, it is difficult to turn around. Future officers in the new, larger unions may find new ways to "secure their offices," thus widening the gap between the members' right to determine and the leaders' autocratic right to proclaim.

Regal Touches

Fortunately, the malaise is not yet that general. But as the UMWA found out in the price it paid while murder was being plotted by leaders among them, we ought to be dealing in preventive medicine. The regality that some unions have permitted themselves, symbolized by the top floor suites of their often plush union headquarters, may represent America's progress but are somewhat inconsistent with the trade unions' role in that growth.

If unions do not change, there will be a growing trend for even the union with only 50,000 members to reward its top officer upon retirement with a $1 million fund for his personal use. This happened in 1973 in one of the maritime trade unions. Will the retiree make his bequest to charity? Will he endow his union? Will he see the world as a touring potentate with big spending habits? A million dollars for one trade union leader?

These are the kinds of questions that the members, widely separate from their leaders in terms of union democracy, were asking when that decision was made.

Communicating Workplace Facts

The participatory democracy of an American trade union will depend upon full use of communication devices that deal with the total workplace as factually as possible. When a person is maimed on the job, will the facts prevail and will such job injury be prevented by members demanding and getting corrective action? If so, participatory democracy is not to be feared—but every potential medium must be brought into play. Questions put to the light make membership decision-making feasible.

If workers are causing inflation by higher wage contracts, will the workers themselves be given the full story by their union officers of what impact a contract will have on the employer and his ability to make an honest profit?

Will the worker understand that he may have to bargain with the employer about the price of the employer's product or service if he understands just what that economic impact is?

Will the worker have at his command the facts through his leadership if his employer, through no fault of his own, is suffering financially? If so, will the worker follow a leadership recommendation of, for instance, a short-term agreement until the employer's financial position can be reviewed again? Or will the worker demand that the leaders be tossed out because the worker has not learned what participatory democracy is all about?

And if the employer is in shaky financial position because of mismanagement, will the worker and his union leader seek to bargain for the revision of the management structure so that the product or service offered by the employer can be competitive?

Limitation on Members' Involvement Weakens Total System

All of these are leading questions, of course. Some people could read into them whole areas of "things that aren't there." They are meant, however, to suggest that trade union democracy at the membership level has failed in so many instances because leaders have felt that their only security in being reelected to their jobs has been to devise a system for their personal benefit. Even if they have otherwise led well, the lack of involvement by members they serve weakens the fiber of the union and its potential service to members, employers, and the public at large.

America's trade unions and their leaders need to give more than lip service to the whole concept of just what a member ought to be doing to participate in his union and just what an officer ought to be doing to make certain that the member can participate without fear or favor.

The last chapter takes one more look at this—for the moment, it must be concluded that most members do not adequately understand the great strengths and values their unions could provide for them, for their employers, and for consumers. Because they don't understand sufficiently well, members either do not often seek or demand the democracy that the trade union structure could offer them.

10

Washing the Linen

Some labor leaders become livid when another union leader makes statements that are publicly critical of either some segment of the labor movement or of some other leaders. "Wash that linen within the family—not in public" is the cry.

Whether or not anyone likes it, trade unionism is quite public. Its whole nature is public. The picket sign is public. It washes the employer's linen, but it invites public retort about the union if the strike or impasse persists.

There are as many styles of labor leadership as there are kinds of leaders. It's easy to define one's own brand of trade unionism and try to make it stand up as if there is only one brand.

No One Trade Union Brand

The point is that there is no one brand of trade unionism. The fact that some of the union leaders see their respective brand as the only one is more at the root of the aversion to washing the linen in public than any factor, in my opinion.

A second factor, of course, is the willingness of anyone who "has it made" to let someone else continue to make it for him.

We do have large sections of affluent union members. We have some large sections that aren't so affluent, too. But it is easy for the trade union member who is relatively comfortable and secure in his material well-being to let his union leader do just about anything he wants. Then, when someone criticizes that leader, even if the leader has become basically undemocratic in serving his affluent membership, the member is quick to defend the leader from criticism.

Separatism Enhances Public Utterance

Linen will be washed in public so long as separatism prevails among major unions in America. This separatism will be increased if membership involvement in union decision-making is stifled or delayed by any means. Either the leaders down under who seek to obtain office and to reform the union will wash the union's linen in public or the growing leadership aristocracy of the separatist unions will wash the movement's linen in their own public utterances condemning each other.

The tug of diversity among trade unions has already demonstrated some of this in the decade of the '70s.

The lowly farm workers and the Teamsters added to the caustic interchanges that the Teamsters' Fitzsimmons and the AFL-CIO's Meany hung out to dry in 1973. If Meany's comments about the leader of the nation's largest union were to be expanded upon by the enemies of labor as an attack upon all of almost 2,000,000 work-productive Teamsters in the country, the linen would be dirtied more, shredded, and difficult to recycle.

This is why some trade unionists want any spokesman to shut up, even when injustice might be at stake. In this case, I see the evidence as clear—the farm worker will be further stooped into the earth unless Meany is able to rally the AFL-CIO rank-and-filer. And how can he do that without speaking out?

Protest Needed for Justice

Someone once said, "To sin by silence when they should protest makes cowards of men." Protest hangs the linen in public view.

It is proper that trade unionists themselves raise the question as to why key blue-collar leadership is not seeking to put together the funding and the know-how to organize white-collar America. Raise the question, and the small, often conservative Office and Professional Employees International Union (OPEIU) leadership will join in the blue-collar lament which fears that some more vigorous leadership, someplace in the union ranks, will focus attention on organizing white-collar workers, who suffer more than many workers from the inflation of the 1970s.

Walter Reuther used to raise the white-collar organizational question in the 1950s and '60s, but he didn't get the job done during his lifetime. Thus, the small office workers union is still protected in the confines of its leadership, which at this point reaches out to far too few.

Linen Piece: Minorities in Unions

Is it proper to wash the linen of only the skilled trades when the subject is minorities in the workplace?

Of course not, but when that linen has been hung out to dry, the inference is that there is some more linen that ought to be hung out, too.

The answer of a trade unionist like myself has been the same kind of defensive answer that all labor leaders must come up with if labor's position is to be justified: "Don't pick on the building trades; better read the record; better look at the outreach programs; better note that there is progress being made. How about the doctors and the lawyers and the architects and the engineers—what are they doing about equal professional opportunity?"

Basically, the answer becomes an unethical one, even if the linen of the professions, if hung out in public view, would look tattletale gray on first view.

There is simply a lot of public controversy that is inevitably going to continue well past the mid '70s when it comes to equal employment opportunity.

No One Measures Up

No one has been measuring up—not government, not business, not the professions, and not labor. But labor is making progress—let's not hang out that linen unless we hang out last week's right alongside—you'll see it is cleaner.

More importantly, even though it is a lot to expect of labor, unions will probably be able to adjust more readily to doing better than other economic segments of our society simply because a union is primarily a people institution, and people institutions, from time to time, demand equal rights for all participants. They have to air their in-house grievances while they are making that demand on their institutions, their leaders, and their fellow members.

The union member or leader who reads this should not fear to open the doors of his union house to public view. As FDR put it, only fear itself is to be feared.

Nothing to Fear Except Continuing Unemployment

If we in organized labor are fearful of washing that linen, then we had best turn our attention to a positive program that tackles the institutions that could provide equal opportunity: government and business.

Labor as a movement could take a cue from the assertion of the former Chancellor of the Federal Republic of Germany, Willy Brandt. In 1974, for the first time, West Germany found that in certain areas of the nation's labor market there were more Germans than jobs "naturally available."

Brandt had stated that the first mission of government is to secure a job for everyone willing, able, and ready for work. "It may require every additional tax penny . . . we will concentrate our efforts on the task of ensuring high employment and maintaining economic growth with price stability. Not everyone will retain his workplace. But government and industry in partnership will bend all efforts to maintain a job for everyone."

Who circulated this statement to every worker in West Germany?—The West German Federation of Labor (DGB), representing over 80 percent of the work force of that nation.

Labor Obligated to Battle for Full Employment

If American labor needs to have its leadership challenge each other about the failure of all America to provide equal employment opportunity, its first task is to fight shoulder to shoulder to demand of government and business full employment—not 4 or 5 or 8 percent or any level of unemployment—for every willing, able, and trainable adult in this nation.

If that drive is the success it could be, then any segment of American labor that consorts with government or business to keep the minorities underemployed needs to be exposed. Some actions among family members warrant public attention.

In the meantime, the unemployed black, brown, red, yellow workers and poor whites are going to bring inadequacies of union leadership to public attention because they see the trade unions as being the basic American institution that ought to be fighting for an economy that gives them decent job opportunities.

Stumbling Blocks and Challenge

In the mid-1970s, the pollsters point out that the business community, labor leadership, and political officeholders are held in low esteem. The principal stumbling block to raising the public's opinion of trade unions is the inadequacy of leadership in far too many segments of the movement.

Why the inadequacy?

For one thing, which institution in America is going to set out a program to train democratic leadership in any institution of the American republic?

The trainer perforce must select who is to be trained. As soon as there is a focus on potential leadership for labor, the anti-union fuss will break out fast. If the trainer is a public institution, like a school, all the more so. If the unions themselves set about it, the internal frictions would be great.

Which institution dares to undertake the risk of selecting and training for democratic institutional leadership within unions? In what direction is the training to go? Is the training to be for lifelong leadership? In the next and final chapter, there is an outline of how this author believes this key stumbling block might be attacked—not overcome—but at least attacked with the purpose of finding the way to overcome.

In the meantime, the unethical practices of institutional trade union leadership will continue to prevail and to do damage. Workers who already have it made will hang onto what they have. Minorities will have to battle hard at the door of the work marketplace. The linen will still be soiled. The challenge is to wash the linen clean.

11

Charting New Courses

Until our economic society finds a better way than having government be an employer and private business be an employer, trade unions are going to be around.

There will be frailities in the union community. But, I believe, unions will be less frail in the decades ahead.

The Arnold Millers are reassuring. There are a number of them already on the scene. Not all appear to be as genuine as the UMWA leader, but they are a better group than the decade of the '60s produced.

Conscience of Leadership

The aristocrats among the labor leadership who have consciences are reassuring. They will not be able to stand much longer the abuses of private gain or personal privilege, no matter how brilliant the leader might be, at the top of the key trade unions of the land. They will move to reform the movement.

Some people feel that today's young generation is no different from any other. They say they will not continue to demand a better way of life. However, there appears to be an increasing number of youths in the job market and in the union halls who question why their voices cannot be heard all the way up and all the way across the trade union structure.

To hear these voices; to invite these voices to take action; to give these voices the facts of workplace and of employer/union conditions; to respond to these knowledgeable demands—this is the challenge that, if answered, will make labor a more participatory democracy.

The times are too perilous to say that it will not happen; the American genius is too widespread to say that workers are not up to demanding these reforms and to putting them into widespread practice even before 1980.

For the leaders already on deck, fear not—it couldn't happen to better people!

Just as Americans have come to learn since 1789 that they can be proud citizens of their home states but first they are Americans, it is equally possible for union members to be proud members of their own unions but basically be trade unionists first. This is the hope for trade union America's future.

What of a New Course?

No new course is going to be undertaken easily.

For one thing, those already well established in trade union structures that seem to be financially secure are not going to drive a new course willingly.

There can always be a minor revolution of leadership—in the case of local unions, where the secret ballot prevails, it has been happening with increasing frequency. But with the big unions of America, it's difficult to get away from the process of the incumbent officers selecting their own successors. The exceptions have been dealt with in this book—the International Typographical Union, the Steelworkers, and the Mine Workers. They are exceptions not because incumbent officers cannot help to find and promote leaders, but more realistically because the secret ballot provides opportunity for a reasonable challenge by a potential group of new leaders who have not been preselected.

In the case of the majority of unions, the top leaders are difficult to unseat; the heirs-apparent are too secure in their ascendancy; it is difficult to generate revolution within most unions because it takes so many people in so many local unions in so many places to stand up and be counted. It also takes time; unfortunately, to most local unions, time is in short supply; they have difficulty in challenging either autocratic or inadequate leadership.

It should be obvious to the reader that I believe the greatest limitation upon the American labor movement to be the great void in democratic practices between the local union and the international union. I repeat what I said in the preface—most workers, including those already in the union halls, do not understand what great potential the union movement has for the good health of the nation.

Likewise, I believe that the continuing growth of the rigid shells of autocracy in which top union leadership encases itself will eventually crush the local unions and thus the trade union structure. Without a foundation, no walls or roof will stand.

While obviously I have hope that working people will have the wisdom to revise their own systems of dealing with the workplace, I believe it is none too early to attack the autocracy of trade unionism wherever it appears. Some people would use the word *discipline* where I say *autocracy*. But I am simply calling it what it is—the ability of top union leadership to lay out policy dictates and procedures without consulting or involving the membership in any way.

Sometimes the members are consulted; they are always consulted where the secret ballot is available both for election of officers and for agreeing upon policy and issues that have an effect on the constitution, bylaws, or general laws of the respective union.

Bigness within itself is not necessarily bad; it is just often overwhelming. Since American labor has fashioned its structure so often to fit the employer it meets at the bargaining table, it often finds it necessary to be as big as the boss. But when bigness monopolizes, it corrupts. And when government permits monopolies to get bigger even when the bigness does not create or perform efficiently, the bigness needs to be attacked. Our history has proved this; unfortunately, unions have had to throw raw, big power on the bargaining table to keep the giants of industry from overpowering workers, growing less and less democratic and more and more autocratic in the process. The two autocracies seem to blend—at least, so the workers are told. But in the process, the worker who is being served in the workplace seems to get more and more detached from the leaders who speak for him.

Arnold Miller and his fellow officers in the Mine Workers are moving to distribute the power of leadership among more persons at every level of the union. I have every confidence that they will prove it can be done, without weakening their union. Given a period of time to work, unless the whole American society collapses around them, they will have strengthened both the democratic processes of their union and the democratic involvement of their members in the total communities in which they live.

If I were to chart a course for American labor in the next half-decade, I would begin with a revision of the process and of the structure. Then, the substance of the issues and the demands that came out of the revised structure would be more honest; would be better understood by both the union merbership and the public at large; and would be directed and moved in a more creative and wholesome manner than anything we have seen.

The ingredients that I propose are simple, although it would not be simple to put them into effect. Institutions and their bureaucracies get entrenched—and that includes those of trade unions.

First, no union leader of any kind could serve in union office unless he were subject to a secret ballot of the membership for which his office speaks. It would not harm the process to limit the term of such elected office to five years, and in the case of regional or nation-wide elections, to provide that such person elected could not serve more than two terms.

I do not believe that all unions will automatically follow this course. It will probably take a public law conceived with an anti-union bias. It has to project the true beauty of democracy—of the leader who must appear before his flock and know that he must speak for them, not for a handful of self-selected colleagues in the same top ranks.

The secret ballot works at the local union level. The gap between there and the top has to be voided.

Second, the trade unions of America should, like the United States of America, delegate certain national and international policy decisions to a unicameral body of leadership democratically elected out of every jurisdiction in the nation. The leadership, while representing the same wide range of union jurisdictions, cannot be effective if it embraces the same leadership personnel who head the respective unions. That would be like having only the governors of the states sitting in Congress even by their own selection out of a conference of governors. That's what America's House of Labor—the AFL-CIO—now has. That's why the gap between the national interest and the local interest in the union halls is out of phase.

This second phase of charting a new course cannot be commanded by law. It could grow out of the reform resulting from secret ballot elections, however.

Even more important, the economically disadvantaged need the opportunity to select a trade union course to move out of the under-employment and low wage pockets that lock them into an often de-spairing society. They might just seek to represent themselves at the bargaining table when they know that their voices will be protected from bottom to top by the choice of a secret ballot. They are given no promise of that now; they move toward unionism out of other desperation. When some union leaders sell them short, even as their employers have done, they are powerless to act; thus, they are not attracted to the system as it is. In fact, they often turn themselves away from the mainstream of all American political and economic society.

Even if these solutions seem logical, they are not simple to achieve. But the nation needs a restoration of democratic spirit in the union halls before it will ever get the restoration that it needs in the 1970s in our political society.

APPENDIX A

Court Decisions
Colorado Labor Council
vs. AFL-CIO

IN THE UNITED STATES DISTRICT COURT
FOR THE DISTRICT OF COLORADO

COLORADO LABOR COUNCIL, AFL-CIO, an unincorporated association, HERRICK ROTH and A. TOFFOLI, Plaintiffs, vs. AMERICAN FEDERATION OF LABOR AND CONGRESS OF INDUSTRIAL ORGANIZATIONS, an unincorporated association, GEORGE MEANY, and DANIEL J. HEALY, Defendants.	CIVIL ACTION NO. C-4342 October 2, 1972

Philip Hornbein, Jr. and Roy O. Goldin, Attorneys at law, Suite 1780, 1600 Broadway, Denver, Colorado, for Plaintiffs; Thomas E. Harris, Associate General Counsel AFL-CIO, 815 16th Street, N.W., Washington, D.C., and MacDonald and Fattor, Of Counsel, by Donald P. MacDonald and rado, for Defendants.
James C. Fattor, Attorneys at law, 555 Capitol Life Center, Denver, Colo-

MEMORANDUM OPINION

WINNER, Judge
This memorandum opinion contains the findings of fact and conclusions of law required by Rule 52 and it is intended to meet the requirements of Rule 65 of the Rules of Civil Procedure.

The amended complaint was filed September 25, 1972, and an answer and counterclaim was filed shortly thereafter. The matter was heard on September 28, 1972, on cross motions for a preliminary injunction.

The Colorado Labor Council is an unincorporated association of labor unions in Colorado. It is affiliated with the American Federation of Labor and Congress of Industrial Organizations, and it is an organization known in labor parlance as a central body. Roth is the president and Toffoli is the secretary-treasurer of the Colorado Labor Council. The American Federation of Labor and Congress of Industrial Organizations is an unincorporated association and it is a labor organization within the meaning of that term as defined in 29 U.S.C. §402 (i). Meany is the president and Healy is a regional director of the AFL-CIO, and Healy has been named by Meany to act as trustee of the Colorado Labor Council.

On July 19, 1972, the AFL-CIO Executive Council adopted this statement:

> "Under the circumstances, the AFL-CIO will refrain from endorsing either candidate for the office of President of the United States.
>
> "Those circumstances call, rather for the maximum concentration of effort upon the election of Senators and Representatives whose records commend them to the working people of America.
>
> *"Affiliates are, of course, free to endorse and support any candidate of their choice."* [emphasis supplied.]

Mr. Meany wrote all state and local central bodies on July 21, 1972, advising them of the Executive Council's policy statement, and he said, "The term 'affiliates' in this policy statement refers only to national and international unions." He reminded them that Rule 4 of the AFL-CIO requires that state and local central bodies conform their activities on national affairs to AFL-CIO policies, and, indeed, the rule says just that. The Colorado Council interpreted the Executive Council's action as permitting endorsement by it of the candidate of the Colorado Council's choice, and Roth urged endorsement of Senator McGovern, as did the Council's Committee on Political Education [COPE]. The next day, by telegram, President Meany reminded the individual plaintiffs of the AFL-CIO Executive Council's action and of his interpretation of the word "affiliates" as used in the Council's policy statement. His telegram said:

> ". . . the Council is in violation of the AFL-CIO Constitution and Rules Governing State Central Bodies and you are hereby directed to take immediate steps to rescind that action and to so advise this office."

The same day, Mr. Roth sent copies of the Colorado resolution to all members of the AFL-CIO Executive Council, to the AFL-CIO Central Bodies and to Mr. Meany. He asked a ruling from Mr. Meany. Shortly after receipt of the letter of August 8, 1972, Mr. Meany advised Roth by telegram that the action of the Colorado body violated the AFL-CIO constitution and rules governing state central bodies, and the telegram said, "The Council is again accordingly hereby directed immediately to rescind its resolution endorsing the McGovern ticket." He set an August 21, 1972, deadline for the taking of the directed action, and he said that if such action were not taken, "I shall have no alternative to instituting disciplinary proceedings against the Council and its officers under the AFL-CIO Constitution and Rules Governing Central Bodies." On August 17, 1972, the Colorado Executive Board refused to comply with President Meany's directives, and preparations for war were commenced.

On the deadline date, a Notice of Hearing was sent by Mr. Meany to the Colorado Council and its officers. The charges were set forth in the hearing notice, and plaintiffs were charged as follows:

"It is charged that the Colorado Labor Council, AFL-CIO, its President, Herrick S. Roth, and its Secretary-Treasurer, A. Toffoli, have violated and failed to comply with Rule 4 of the Rules Governing AFL-CIO State Central Bodies, and that they have engaged in a course of conduct which is detrimental to the best interests of the AFL-CIO, and have failed to conform the policies of the Colorado Labor Council, AFL-CIO, to the policies of the AFL-CIO.

"These charges are based on the following specifics:

"On July 19, 1972, the AFL-CIO Executive Council resolved that the AFL-CIO would not endorse either candidate for President of the United States. The President of the AFL-CIO advised the Colorado Labor Council of this action, and further advised it that, while national and international unions affiliated with the AFL-CIO were free to endorse any candidate of their choice, this freedom did not extend to AFL-CIO state or local central bodies, which as subordinate bodies of the AFL-CIO, were required to conform their policies on national affairs to those of the AFL-CIO. President Roth and Secretary-Treasurer Toffoli nevertheless continued to take the position that Colorado COPE was free to make an endorsement and to urge that it endorse Senator McGovern. On August 7, 1972, the Committee on Political Education of the Colorado Labor Council, AFL-CIO, adopted a resolution endorsing Senator McGovern for President. It also adopted a motion that the resolution be submitted to the President of the AFL-CIO for his ruling under Rule 4.

"Thereafter, the President of the AFL-CIO again advised the Colorado Labor Council that AFL-CIO state and local central bodies are not permitted to endorse any candidate for President and that the Colorado Labor Council endorsement of Senator McGovern placed it in violation of the AFL-CIO Constitution and Rules and must be rescinded. Notwithstanding these communications from the President of the AFL-CIO, the Colorado Labor Council, AFL-CIO, has not rescinded its endorsement of Senator McGovern."

The hearing notice designated hearing officers and fixed a hearing date which was later continued at the request of Mr. Roth to August 30, 1972. The press was excluded from the hearing, counsel were not allowed to participate, and, to put it mildly, a review of the transcript of those proceedings convinces that the command of the United States Supreme Court in *New York Times v. Sullivan* (1964) 376 U.S. 254, was obeyed to its fullest. The comment to which we refer is that which says that we have "a profound national commitment to the principle that debate on public issues should be uninhibited, robust, and wide-open, and it may well include vehement, caustic, and sometimes unpleasantly sharp attacks (on others)."

The hearing officers prepared a written report and submitted it to President Meany on September 15, 1972. The full report is an exhibit in the case and it concluded:

"On the basis of the evidence adduced at the hearing and summarized herein, we find that the Colorado Labor Council, AFL-CIO, its President, Herrick S. Roth, and its Secretary-Treasurer, A. Toffoli, have violated and failed to comply with Rule 4 of the Rules Governing AFL-CIO State Central Bodies, and that they have engaged in a course of conduct which is detrimental to the best interests of the AFL-CIO, and have failed to conform to the policies of the Colorado Labor Council, AFL-CIO, to the policies of the AFL-CIO." (sic)

Four days later, President Meany signed his Decision and Order which approved and accepted the hearing officers' report. The decision ordered suspension of the Colorado Council, the individual plaintiffs here, and all members of the Executive Board of the Colorado Council. The defendant Healy was appointed trustee "to take charge of and conduct the business of the Colorado Labor Council." This lawsuit followed, and in it plaintiffs ask the Court to enjoin the trusteeship, and defendants counterclaim and ask injunctive relief requiring recognition by the plaintiffs of the trusteeship and ask the Court to order plaintiffs to comply with the orders issued to them by Mr. Meany. In the meantime, the parties have been operating under a sort of armed truce awaiting this Court's decision, and the need for immediate decision is emphasized by the fact that a convention of the Colorado Labor Council has been called for October 4, 1972. If we hold that the trusteeship is valid, the trustee will call off the convention; if we hold the trusteeship is invalid, the convention will go forward under the aegis of Roth, Toffoli and the Executive Board of the Colorado Council.

In this case, there is but one issue, and matters not in dispute should be separated from it:—

1. Neither the Colorado Labor Council nor the AFL-CIO claims any right to, (a) dictate or control anyone's vote; (b) curtail any individual's freedom to voice any political views he or she may have, or (c) control the endorsement by any labor union [as distinguished from a central body] of any political candidate, including presidential candidates.

2. The AFL-CIO claims no right to restrict political endorsements by central bodies, except endorsements by those bodies of candidates for President and Vice-President.

3. The Colorado Labor Council asks only that it be permitted to attempt to persuade—not to intimidate, dominate or control voters in the marking of their presidential ballot.

4. The Colorado Labor Council says that it has, and the AFL-CIO says that the Council does not have a present right to endorse a presidential ticket. This is the only dispute before us, albeit the parties attack the problem with an imposing array of arguments, only one of which we today resolve.

Although we today decide only one of the arguments, we summarize the contentions made simply to demonstrate the complexity of the situation.

The Colorado Labor Council argues that it is subject to the provisions of the Labor-Management Reporting and Disclosure Act of 1959; that the bill of rights of that act is fully applicable, and that a trusteeship can be imposed on it only if the tests of 29 U.S.C. §462 [Sec. 302 of the Act] are met. The section provides:

> "Trusteeships shall be established and administered by a labor organization over a subordinate body only in accordance with the constitution and bylaws of the organization which has assumed trusteeship over the subordinate body and for the purpose of correcting corruption or financial malpractice, assuring the performance of collective bargaining agreements or other duties of a bargaining representative, restoring democratic procedures, or otherwise carrying out the legitimate objects of such labor organizations."

Additionally, 29 U.S.C. §464 (c) says that when, after a fair hearing, a trusteeship is established by a labor organization in accordance with the procedural requirements of its constitution and bylaws, the trusteeship shall be presumed valid for a period of 18 months and that it can be upset only "upon clear and convincing proof that the trusteeship was not established or maintained in good faith for a purpose allowable under Sec. 302 (of the Act)." Here, the "purpose allowable under Sec. 302," of the Act is said by defendants to be, "otherwise carrying out the legitimate objects of such labor organization."

Plaintiffs take these positions:

1.   The trusteeship was not created on any ground set forth in Sec. 302 of the Act.

2.   The action taken by the AFL-CIO was not taken in accordance with the constitution and bylaws of the AFL-CIO.

3.   The trusteeship was ordered without complying with the requirements of 29 U.S.C. §464 (c) requiring a fair hearing.

4.   Plaintiffs' right to endorse a presidential candidate of their choice is a right protected by the First Amendment, by the Bill of Rights of the Labor-Management Reporting and Disclosure Act [29 U.S.C. §411] and by the Constitution of the AFL-CIO.

5.   The action of the AFL-CIO Executive Council did not prohibit the endorsement of Senator McGovern by the Colorado Labor Council.

In answer, defendants say:

1.   There are contractual relationships between the AFL-CIO and the Colorado Labor Council resulting from the AFL-CIO Constitution, the Rules Governing AFL-CIO State Central Bodies and the Charter issued by the AFL-CIO to the Colorado Labor Council. Defendants say that the Colorado Labor Council has by contract agreed to permit the AFL-CIO to have exclusive jurisdiction over the endorsement of candidates for the offices of President and Vice-President of the United States, and, say defendants, the action of the Colorado Labor Council violates the agreements between the parties.

2.   The hearing afforded plaintiffs was fair, and the action of the AFL-CIO Executive Council was fair.

3.   The actions of President Meany were authorized, and he had a right to define the word "affiliates."

4.   The Colorado Labor Council violated Rule 4 in that it engaged in a course of conduct detrimental to the best interests of the AFL-CIO and in that it failed to conform its policies to those of the AFL-CIO.

5.   The trusteeship has been lawfully created, and defendants are entitled to injunctive relief on their counterclaim to enforce the trusteeship.

We first face up to a threshold jurisdictional question. In their complaint, plaintiffs say jurisdiction is founded on 29 U.S.C. §412 and §464, and on 28 U.S.C. §1337. Defendants admit jurisdiction in their answer. However, as part of their argument, defendants say that although the AFL-CIO is a labor organization, the Colorado Labor Council is not.[1] Moreover, say defendants, 29 U.S.C. §464 is not applicable to the Colorado Labor Council. This argument rests on defendants' interpretation of the Congressional Record while the Bill was under consideration by the Senate and the House and upon a claimed compromise reached between Senators Kennedy and Goldwater as to the impact and coverage of this section. We leave for later determination the resolution of this question, should such determination become necessary. However, 29 U.S.C. §412 confers jurisdiction over any

[1]Defendants say that they are a labor organization, because the AFL-CIO constitution makes some labor unions affiliates.

claim of infringement of rights granted by the Act, §462 of that title men-
tions trusteeships established by a labor organization "over a subordinate
body," §463 has to do with trusteeships of a "subordinate body of a labor
organization;" §464 gives jurisdiction to the Court over any suit brought by
a member of a subordinate body of a labor organization affected by a violation of the Act, and 29 U.S.C. §464 is one of the Act's sections relied on
most strongly by defendants because of its statutory presumptions of validity
of trusteeships. On final argument, plaintiffs' counsel emphatically asserted
jurisdiction, while defendants' counsel were wishy-washy and refused to take
a position on the question. Again without determination at this time as to
whether the Colorado Labor Council is a labor organization for trusteeship
purposes under the Act, it is undeniably a subordinate body of a labor
organization, and we find and conclude that we do have jurisdiction of the
case.

Defendants argue that totally apart from any provisions of the Labor-
Management Act, the AFL-CIO has a right to impose the present trusteeship. They point out that the Colorado Labor Council has agreed to abide by
the rules of the AFL-CIO; that Rule 4 says that state central bodies "shall
conform their activities on national affairs to the policies of the AFL-CIO,"
and that they shall "assist in furthering the appropriate objects and policies
of the AFL-CIO." Rule 25 authorizes the president to take disciplinary action against state central bodies and its officers "when such organization or
officer violates or fails to comply with any of the provisions of the Constitution of the AFL-CIO or of these rules." If disciplinary action is taken, notice
and hearing is required, and Rule 25 says, "The decision of the President
shall be in full force and effect unless or until reversed or changed upon
appeal as provided in paragraph (g) of this rule." Provision is made for
appeal of presidential disciplinary decisions to the Executive Council and
from the Executive Council to the next convention of the AFL-CIO.[2] The
bylaws of Colorado COPE say that "it shall operate in conformity with the
policies of the national AFL-CIO and its national Committee on Political
Education," and the model bylaws provide, "Endorsement of candidates for
President and Vice-President shall be made by the AFL-CIO. The State
COPE shall follow the endorsement of the national AFL-CIO." Colorado-
COPE's bylaws say that "it shall operate in conformity with the policies of
the national AFL-CIO and AFL-CIO COPE." Additionally, they say, "Endorsement of candidates for President and Vice-President shall be made by
the national AFL-CIO. The Colorado COPE shall follow the endorsement
of the national AFL-CIO."

It is upon these and other similar constitutional, by-law and rule provisions that defendants rest their argument that plaintiffs have contractually
agreed to confer exclusive jurisdiction on the AFL-CIO to endorse candidates for President and Vice-President of the United States. Defendants rely

---

[2]With the national election set for five weeks from now, these appeal provisions afford little or no chance for relief to plaintiffs.

on *Letter Carriers v. Sombrotto* (1971) 2 Cir. 449 F. 2d 915 and *Parks v. IBEW* (1963) 4 Cir. 314 F. 2d 886.

Defendants also argue that plaintiffs' suit is premature because they have failed to exhaust their remedies within the union. This argument we reject on authority of *United Brotherhood of Carpenters and Joiners of America v. Brown* (1965) 10 Cir. 343 F. 2d 872. Judge Hill there said:

> "Appellants also contend that the judgment must be reversed and the action dismissed for the reason that the plaintiffs have failed to exhaust the internal remedies afforded by the United Brotherhood's Constitution and Laws as required by section 101 (a) (4) of the Act. 29 U.S.C. §411 (a) (4). We do not agree. Section 101 (a) (4) is applicable only where individual violations of the so-called Bill of Rights provisions are alleged *and does not apply where, as here, the validity of a trusteeship is being challenged.*" [emphasis supplied.]

Plaintiffs say that the hearing is fairly comparable to the trial of the mouse in Alice in Wonderland—" 'I'll be judge, I'll be jury,' said cunning old Fury; 'I'll try the whole cause and condemn you to death,' " and plaintiffs say that the hearing was a nullity because of its inherent unfairness. Defendants say that *Parks v. IBEW*, supra, answers and rejects plaintiffs' arguments concerning the fairness of the hearing.

At the time of the hearing plaintiffs did not press their First Amendment claims, and, although they did not withdraw them, they acknowledged that under cases such as *Reid v. McDonnell Douglas Corp.* (1971) 10 Cir. 443 F. 2d 410, these claims are tenuous. This acknowledgment, of course, went only to the First Amendment claims and plaintiffs did not in any way retreat from their claims under the statutory Bill of Rights.

Finally, defendants argue that the right to control the internal affairs of the AFL-CIO and its affiliated subordinates should be equated to cases involving the right of churches to control their affairs and their doctrine. Defendants here rely on *Watson v. Jones* (1871) 13 Wall 679; *Kedroff v. St. Nicholas Cathedral* (1952) 344 U.S. 94, and *Presbyterian Church v. Hull Church* (1968) 393 U.S. 440. Undeniably, in *Watson v. Jones* it was held:

> "The right to organize voluntary religious associations to create tribunals for the decisions of controverted questions of faith within the association and for the ecclesiastical government of all the individual members of congregations and officers within the general association is unquestioned. All who unite themselves to such a body do so with an implied consent to this government and are bound to submit to it."

As we reach our immediate problem, we pay tribute to the skill of counsel in the preparation of their able briefs and arguments in the extremely limited time available to them, but we are fully aware of the fact that neither the Court nor counsel have had adequate time to fully research the many troublesome questions presented. For that reason, rather than to shoot from the hip, we reserve judgment on almost all of those questions, and on these cross-applications for preliminary injunctions, we decide only those questions necessary to determine our jurisdiction [including the exhaustion of remedies question] and a single question which permits a ruling on a temporary injunction.

Preliminary injunctions have been likened to the issuance of an execution before judgment or to a judgment or execution before trial. *American Smelting and Refining Co. v. Godfrey* 8 Cir. 158 F. 225; 42 *Am. Jur. 2d, Injunctions*, §13, p. 741. Their purpose is to preserve the status quo, and the status quo to be preserved is the last status which existed before the controversy arose. *Steggles v. National Discount Corp.* 326 Mich. 44, 39 N.W. 2d 237. See annotation, 15 *A.L.R. 2d* 237, §4. The Tenth Circuit said in *Continental Oil v. Frontier Refining Company* (1964) 338 F. 2d 780:

> "The function of a preliminary injunction is to preserve the status quo pending a final determination of the rights of the parties. It should be issued only where the plaintiff makes out a prima facie case showing a reasonable probability that he will ultimately be entitled to the relief sought and that irreparable damage will possibly result if the relief is not granted pendente lite. But it has been said that '. . . To justify a temporary injunction it is not necessary that the plaintiff's right to a final decision, after a trial, be absolutely certain, wholly without doubt; if the other elements are present (i.e., the balance of hardships tips decidedly toward plaintiff), it will ordinarily be enough that the plaintiff has raised questions going to the merits so serious, substantial, difficult and doubtful, as to make them a fair ground for litigation and thus for more deliberate investigation.' "

More recently, the Tenth Circuit said in *Crowther v. Seaborg* (1969) 415 F. 2d 437:

> "In hearings upon motions for temporary or preliminary injunctive relief, the burden is upon the one requesting such relief to make a prima facie case showing a reasonable probability that he will ultimately be entitled to the relief sought. The applicant has the additional burden of showing a right to the specific injunctive relief sought because of irreparable injury that will result if the injunction is not granted. There must exist a probable right and a probable danger."

Moreover, in passing upon defendants' cross-motion for a preliminary injunction, because such injunctions are designed to preserve the status quo, mandatory as opposed to prohibitive relief is seldom granted.

In comparing the hardships involved, the scales tip decidedly in plaintiffs' favor. The record establishes that the Colorado Labor Council and its suspended officers have contributed through its programs not only to the labor movement but to the general welfare of the State of Colorado. It is actively engaged in programs designed to alleviate some of the gravest problems confronting our country today. Chancellor Mitchell of the University of Denver emphasized the contributions being made to the State's welfare by plaintiffs, and whether those programs could or would be continued by defendant Healy is unclear from the record. There is a definite public interest in the continuation of these programs, and public interest, of course, is a factor to be weighed by a court in passing on an application for a preliminary injunction. Additionally, the convention of the Colorado Labor Council has already been called and it will open day after tomorrow. And we remind that the United States Supreme Court said in *Williams v. Rhodes* (1968) 393 U.S. 23:

> "The right of individuals to associate for the advancement of political beliefs ranks among our most precious freedoms."

Except for our preliminary determinations that we have jurisdiction and that the suit is not barred under the exhaustion of remedies doctrine, we come to the question of the validity of President Meany's interpretation of the word "affiliates," and all other questions we reserve to be answered on final hearing of this matter. Article III of the AFL-CIO Constitution is entitled "Affiliates," and Section 1 thereof says:

> "The Federation shall be composed of (1) affiliated national and international unions and organizing committees, (2) directly affiliated local unions (such as Local Trade Unions, Federal Labor Unions, and Local Industrial Unions) and national councils thereof, (3) state and local central bodies (such as State and Territorial Federations, City Central Labor Unions and Industrial Union Councils), and (4) trade and industrial departments."

Section 5 of that same Constitutional article says:

> ". . . Local Central Bodies affiliated with the American Federation of Labor at the time of the adoption of this Constitution, and State and Local Industrial Union Councils affiliated with the Congress of Industrial Organizations at the time of this constitution [CLC comes within this definition] *shall become and be affiliates of this Federation . . .*"

By AFL-CIO constitutional definition, then, the Colorado Labor Council is an *affiliate* of the American Federation of Labor and the Congress of Industrial Organizations. In the July 19, 1972, policy statement of the Executive Council of the AFL-CIO it was spelled out that:

> "Affiliates are, of course, free to endorse and support any candidate of their choice."

It is hornbook law that words are presumed to be used in their ordinary meaning, and where words are defined in an organization's constitution, they must be presumed to be used by that organization as it has defined them. These presumptions were called to the attention of defendants' counsel during final argument, and the Court offered defendants an opportunity to reopen their case to present any expert testimony they wished as to a trade or union rule or custom applying a different meaning to the word "affiliate" in matters involving trusteeships or political endorsements. The Court's invitation to present such testimony was not accepted.

Defendants argue that President Meany is empowered to interpret AFL-CIO rules, but we are not talking about a rule. We are talking about the meaning of a constitutionally defined word. Nor are we talking about an interpretation. We are talking about the application of a meaning diametric to the constitutionally defined meaning. Power to interpret is not power to make complete change. President Meany's interpretation of the word "affiliates" amounted to an attempted amendment of the AFL-CIO Constitution. He has no power to individually amend the organization's constitution, and the Executive Council's policy statement must be read to use the word "affiliates" as that word is used in the AFL-CIO Constitution. Had the Executive Council intended to grant the freedom to endorse to a limited type of affiliates it could have easily said so, and surely the Executive Council of the AFL-CIO must have known how that word is defined in the constitution. [We hasten to add that by this comment we express no opinion as to whether any such limitation by the Executive Council would or would not be valid. We say only that the Executive Council did not so limit the right of freedom to endorse, and its power to do so is not before us.] On argument, counsel suggested that this is what the members of Council had in mind. If so, it is not what the Council said, and we know of no authority which permits a Court to engage in mind reading.

With what we have said, then, not only do the scales tip strongly in plaintiffs' favor when the hardships are put in balance, but, additionally, plaintiffs have shown "a probable right and a probable [actually an existing] danger." We believe that plaintiffs have satisfied the requirements of *Continental Oil Company v. Frontier Refining Company,* supra, and *Crowther v. Seaborg,* supra. We must and we shall comply with the command of Rule 65 and of *Atomic Oil Company of Oklahoma v. Bardahl Oil Company* (1970) 10 Cir. 419 F. 2d 1097:

> "Rule 65(c) states in mandatory language that the giving of security is an absolute condition precedent to the issuance of a preliminary injunction."

The bond, of course, must be conditioned "for the payment of such costs and damages as may be incurred or suffered by any party who is found to have been wrongfully enjoined or restrained."

Accordingly, defendants' motion for a preliminary injunction is denied and plaintiffs' motion for a preliminary injunction is granted.

Pending further order of this Court, defendants, and each of them, and all persons acting in concert with them, acting in reliance on the rights and claims asserted by them in this action, are hereby enjoined from taking control, or attempting to take control, of the Colorado Labor Council, its records, assets, offices, employees, affairs or operations by means of imposition of a trusteeship upon the Colorado Labor Council and from interfering or attempting to interfere with the official acts or actions of the officers of the Colorado Labor Council and the members of its Executive Board and with the conduct of the business of the Colorado Labor Council.

This injunction shall become effective upon the posting of bond with the Clerk of this Court in the amount of $5,000.00, such bond to be adequately secured, and to be conditioned as required by Rule 65(c) of the Federal Rules of Civil Procedure.

Dated at Denver, Colorado, this 2nd day of October, 1972.

FRED M. WINNER
United States District Judge

UNITED STATES COURT OF APPEALS
TENTH CIRCUIT
MAY TERM — 1973

COLORADO LABOR COUNCIL, AFL-CIO, an unincorporated association, HERRICK ROTH and A. TOFFOLI,
         Plaintiffs-Appellees,
 v.
 AMERICAN FEDERATION OF LABOR AND CONGRESS OF INDUSTRIAL ORGANIZATIONS, an unincorporated association, GEORGE MEANY and DANIEL J. HEALY,
         Defendants-Appellants.
	NO. 72-1701
	 June 20, 1973

Appeal from the United States District Court
For the District of Colorado
(D.C. No. C-4342)

Philip Hornbein, Jr. (Roy O. Goldin with him on the brief), for Plaintiffs-Appellees.

Thomas E. Harris, Associate General Counsel, AFL-CIO (J. Albert Woll, General Counsel, AFL-CIO, Robert C. Mayer, Laurence Gold, Donald P.

MacDonald and James C. Fattor, with him on the brief), for Defendants-Appellants.

Harlington Wood, Jr., Assistant Attorney General, James L. Treece, United States Attorney, Morton Hollander and William Kanter, Attorneys, Department of Justice; and Richard F. Schubert, Solicitor of Labor, Beate Bloch, Associate Solicitor, Harper Barnes, Regional Solicitor, and Cornelius S. Donoghue, Jr., Attorney, Department of Labor, of Counsel, on the brief, on behalf of the *Secretary of Labor*, as Amicus Curiae.

Before LEWIS, Chief Judge, and BREITENSTEIN and McWILLIAMS, Circuit Judges.

PER CURIAM.

This is an appeal from a preliminary injunction issued by the United States District Court for the District of Colorado prohibiting the effectuation of a trusteeship sought to be imposed by the AFL-CIO over the Colorado Labor Council. In our view, the trial court had no jurisdiction over the subject matter sought to be litigated and accordingly lacked jurisdiction to enter the injunctive order here complained of. Resolution of the controversy involves a consideration of the Labor-Management Reporting and Disclosure Act of 1959, hereinafter referred to as the Act. Some background information is needed if the narrow issue here to be decided is to be placed in focus.

The AFL-CIO is an unincorporated association, headquartered in Washington, D.C., whose membership is composed of affiliated national and international unions, local unions, state and local central bodies, and trade and industrial departments. As concerns state and local central bodies, the Rules of the AFL-CIO provide that state and local central bodies which are granted charters by the AFL-CIO shall conform their activities on national affairs to the policies of the AFL-CIO.

The Colorado Labor Council, hereinafter referred to as the Council, is an unincorporated association chartered by the AFL-CIO in 1956 and headquartered in Denver, Colorado, with its membership being composed of national and international unions affiliated with the AFL-CIO and operating in Colorado, and as such the Council is a state central body.

Without going into great detail, sometime in July 1972, a controversy arose between the AFL-CIO and the Council concerning the endorsement of a candidate for the office of President of the United States. AFL-CIO, on the one hand, determined not to endorse any candidate for the office, but at the same time permitted "affiliates" to endorse any candidate of their choice. By subsequent statement, "affiliates" were declared by the AFL-CIO to be only national and international unions, and not state and local central bodies, such as the Council. The Council, however, interpreted the foregoing pronouncements from its parent body to mean that it was free to endorse a candidate of its choice, notwithstanding the clarification pronouncement that it was not considered to be an affiliate. Accordingly, the Council on August 7, 1972, adopted a resolution endorsing the candidacy of Senator George McGovern for President.

Based on the foregoing events, AFL-CIO instituted internal disciplinary proceedings against the Council, which culminated in a suspension of the Council's charter and the appointment of a trustee to take charge of and conduct the business of the Council in place of its duly elected officials, the latter being suspended from office. When the trustee arrived in Denver, Colorado, prepared to assume control of the Council as trustee, the Council rejected the trusteeship and brought suit in the United States District Court for the State of Colorado seeking to enjoin the imposition of the trusteeship.

Council's complaint was based upon Sections 302 and 304 of the Act, and it was alleged that the proposed imposition of a trusteeship over the Council by the AFL-CIO was in contravention of the provisions of the aforesaid Sections 302 and 304 of the Act. Jurisdiction was based upon those sections of the Act and also upon 28 U.S.C. §1337. After an evidentiary hearing, the trial court determined that it had jurisdiction and entered a preliminary injunction enjoining the AFL-CIO from imposing a trusteeship on the Council. Pursuant to the provisions of 23 U.S.C. §1292(a), AFL-CIO now seeks review of that injunctive order. As indicated, we are of the view that the trial court lacked jurisdiction over the subject matter of the controversy and accordingly was without jurisdiction to enter the preliminary injunction here complained of.

In arguing that the trial court had jurisdiction over the subject matter of the controversy between the parties to the end that the trial court had the requisite jurisdiction to enter the injunctive relief prayed for, the Council, as indicated relies primarily on Sections 302[1] and 304[2] of Title III of the Act as conferring such jurisdiction.

Before considering the several sections of Title III, it would be well to

[1]"Sec. 302. Trusteeships shall be established and administered by a labor organization over a *subordinate body* only in accordance with the constitution and bylaws of the organization which has assumed trusteeship over the *subordinate* body and for the purpose of correcting corruption or financial malpractice, assuring the performance of collective bargaining agreements or other duties of a bargaining representative, restoring democratic procedures, or otherwise carrying out the legitimate objects of such labor organization." (Emphasis added.)

[2]"Sec. 304. (a) Upon the written complaint of any member or *subordinate body* of a labor organization alleging that such organization has violated the provisions of this title (except section 301) the Secretary shall investigate the complaint and if the Secretary finds probable cause to believe that such violation has occurred and has not been remedied he shall, without disclosing the identity of the complainant, bring a civil action in any district court of the United States having jurisdiction of the labor organization for such relief (including injunctions) as may be appropriate. Any member or *subordinate body* of a labor organization affected by any violation of this title (except section 301) may bring a civil action in any district court of the United States having jurisdiction of the labor organization for such relief (including injunctions) as may be appropriate." (Emphasis added.)

bear in mind one of the several definitions appearing in the preamble to the Act itself. The phrase "labor organization" is first carefully defined in considerable detail in affirmative language, and then the definition concludes with the negative language that a "labor organization" is something "other than a state or local central body." In this regard, counsel are in apparent agreement that that the Council is a state central body and not a "labor organization," as the latter is defined in the Act.

The fact that the Council is not a "labor organization" as defined in the Act goes to the heart of the controversy. In this regard, AFL-CIO and the Secretary of Labor, as amicus curiae, contend that the provisions of Title III relating to the imposition of a trusteeship by a labor organization contemplate only the imposition of a trusteeship by a parent labor organization over a subordinate labor organization and have no application to the situation where, as here, a labor organization attempts to impose a trusteeship over a state central body, since the latter is not a labor organization.

The Council argues that on the contrary, Sections 302 and 304 refer to the imposition of a trusteeship by a labor organization over a "subordinate body" and that the Council, being a subordinate body to the AFL-CIO, is entitled to avail itself of the limitations placed on the imposition of a trusteeship by Section 302 and of the provisions of Section 304 permitting a subordinate body to seek injunctive relief in the federal district court. In rejoinder to this particular argument, the AFL-CIO counters that if the phrase "subordinate body," as used in Sections 302 and 304 of the Act, be read in context, then the phrase "subordinate body" means "subordinate labor organization." We agree with this latter interpretation.

Counsel for both sides rely to some extent on the legislative history of the Act as supporting their particular interpretation of Title III. We regard the legislative history to be inconclusive, and prefer to resolve the matter on the basis of the Act itself. In reaching the conclusion that Title III is concerned only with the imposition of a trusteeship by a labor organization over a subordinate labor organization, and does not concern itself with the imposition of a trusteeship over a subordinate body such as a state central body, we are influenced by the following factors:

1.   As indicated, in the definition section of the Act, the phrase "labor organization" is defined, inter alia, as being something "other than a state or local central body." The Act consists of six titles, and it is undisputed that Titles I, II, IV, V and VI have no application to state central bodies. In such circumstance we are disinclined to hold that out of the entire Act, Title III alone, and only two sections at that, has application to state central bodies, in the absence of a clear and unmistakable legislative intent that such was in fact intended. We find no such clear and unmistakable legislative intendment.

2.   Section 301[3] of Title III by its express terms clearly applies only in

[3]"Sec. 301. (a) Every labor organization which has or assumes trusteeship over any *subordinate labor organiaztion* shall file with the Secretary within thirty days after the date of any such trusteeship, and semiannually thereafter, a report,

the case of a trusteeship imposed on a subordinate labor organization, with that particular section requiring periodic accounting by the parent body when it imposes a trusteeship on a subordinate labor organization. Such being the case, it is difficult for us to understand why Congress would not similarly provide that when a labor organization imposes a trusteeship over a "subordinate body," such as a state central body, it must also make a periodic accounting of its trusteeship. Yet such is clearly not the case. So, assuming for the moment that Sections 302 and 304 of Title III be held to encompass state central bodies, as well as subordinate labor organizations, then in the case of a trusteeship over a subordinate labor organization the parent body must make a periodic accounting, but when it imposes a trusteeship over a subordinate body, such as a state central body, it need not make any periodic accounting. We do not believe that Congress intended any such different handling, all of which leads us to conclude that it was not the intent of Congress to include state central bodies under the coverage of any section of Title III.

3. Section 303[4] of Title III uses the phrase "labor organization under trusteeship" in its heading. Hence, we assume, and with justification we believe, that the body of Section 303 is concerned with, and limited to,

---

signed by its president and treasurer or corresponding principal officers, as well as by the trustees of such subordinate labor organization, containing the following information: (1) the name and address of the *subordinate organization;* (2) the date of establishing the trusteeship; (3) a detailed statement of the reason or reasons for establishing or continuing the trusteeship; and (4) the nature and extent of participation by the membership of the *subordinate organization* in the selection of delegates to represent such organization in regular or special conventions or other policydetermining bodies and in the election of officers of the labor organization which has assumed trusteeship over such *subordinate organization.* The initial report shall also include a full and complete account of the financial condition of such *subordinate organization* as of the time trusteeship was assumed over it. During the continuance of a trusteeship the labor organization which has assumed trusteeship over a *subordinate labor organization* shall file on behalf of the subordinate labor organization the annual financial report required by section 201(b) signed by the president and treasurer or corresponding principal officers of the labor organization which has assumed such trusteeship and the trustees of the subordinate labor organization." (Emphasis added.)

[4]"Unlawful Acts Relating to *Labor Organizations under Trusteeship.*

"Sec. 303. (a) During any period when a *subordinate body* of a labor organization is in trusteeship, it shall be unlawful (1) to count the vote of delegates from such body in any convention or election of officers of the labor organization unless the delegates have been chosen by secret ballot in an election in which all the members in good standing of such *subordinate* body were eligible to participate or (2) to transfer to such organization any current receipts or other funds of the *subordinate body* except the normal per capita tax and assessments payable by *subordinate bodies* not in trusteeship: *Provided,* That nothing herein contained shall prevent the distribution of the assets of a *labor organization* in accordance with its constitution and bylaws upon the bona fide dissolution thereof." (Emphasis added.)

"labor organizations under trusteeship." Nevertheless, the phrase "subordinate body" is used in the body of that section four times and then a switch is made and the phrase "labor organization" is next and last used in the proviso clause. Thus the two phrases "labor organization under trusteeship" and "subordinate body" are used, in a very real sense we submit, interchangeably in Section 303. Such suggests to us quite strongly that Congress contemplated that the "subordinate body" under trusteeship would be a "subordinate labor organization."

We concede that the Council in a literal sense is a "subordinate body" of the AFL-CIO. However, the Supreme Court has cautioned against a literal reading of labor legislation in general, and the Act in particular. *Wirtz v. Bottle Blowers Association,* 389 U.S. 463 (1968). And for the reasons above stated we are of the firm view that Sections 302 and 304 of Title III should not be read literally, and that, when read in context, the phrase "subordinate body" as used in those two sections means, and is limited to, "subordinate labor organizations."

The Council also contends that regardless of the construction given Sections 302 and 304 of the Act, the trial court nonetheless had subject matter jurisdiction by virtue of the provisions of 23 U.S.C. §1337.[5] In this regard, it has been held that although §1337 confers jurisdiction, it does not in and of itself create a cause of action. *See,* for example, *B. F. Goodrich Company v. Northwest Industries, Inc.,* 424 F. 2d 1349 (3d Cir. 1970). Assuming that the requirements of §1337 were otherwise met, it is clear to us that the action which the Council seeks to maintain in nowise arises under the Act. For the reasons set forth above, we have held to the contrary. Accordingly, §1337 does not in and of itself confer jurisdiction upon the trial court to enter the preliminary injunction here complained of.

The Third Circuit, in a factual situation akin to that of the instant one, has quite recently reached the same result as have we and on similar reasoning. *New Jersey County and Municipal Council No. 61 v. American Federation of State, County and Municipal Employees,* _____ F. 2d _____, their case No. 72-1645, decided May 4, 1973. There, as here, the trial court enjoined the effectuation of a trusteeship by a parent labor organization over a subordinate body which, under the Act, was not a labor organization. There, the subordinate body over which the trusteeship was sought to be imposed was not a state central body, but a local union which limited its membership to *public* employees and accordingly under the terms of the Act was not a labor organization. In such setting, the Third Circuit stated that the "only conclusion which we can reasonably reach is that public employee unions are not covered by the phrase 'subordinate body' in §§302 and 304." Accordingly, the Third Circuit reversed the trial court on the ground that under the circumstances it had "no subject matter jurisdiction."

The preliminary injunction heretofore entered by the trial court is ac-

[5]"The district courts shall have jurisdiction of any civil action or proceeding arising under any act of Congress regulating commerce or protective trade and commerce against restraints and monopolies."

cordingly vacated and the cause is now remanded to the trial court with directions to dismiss the action.

UNITED STATES COURT OF APPEALS
TENTH CIRCUIT
No. 72-1701

COLORADO LABOR COUNCIL, AFL-
CIO, an unincorporated association, HER-
RICK ROTH and A. TOFFOLI,
                              Plaintiffs-Appellees,
v.

AMERICAN FEDERATION OF LABOR
AND CONGRESS OF INDUSTRIAL
ORGANIZATIONS, an unincorporated
association, GEORGE MEANY and
DANIEL J. HEALY,
                              Defendants-Appellants.

On Appeal from the United States District Court
for the District of Colorado
(D.C. No. C-4342)

PETITION FOR REHEARING
JULY 3, 1973

In this petition for rehearing, plaintiffs-appellees do not ask this Court to reconsider its decision that sec. 302, LMRDA [29 USC §462], is applicable only to subordinate labor organizations and that the Colorado Labor Council therefore is not entitled to the benefit of its provisions. We request only that the Court reconsider its judgment vacating the District Court's preliminary injunction, and directing the District Court to dismiss the action, and in support of this petition, we respectfully show the Court:

1. In addition to their claim for relief under secs. 302 and 304, LMRDA [29 USC §§462, 464], plaintiffs also asserted a claim for relief under secs. 101(a) (2) and 102 [the Bill of Rights] of the Act, 29 USC §§411 and 412 [Amended Complaint, pars. 1, 10 and 12].

2. Plaintiffs seek relief under secs. 101(a) (2) and 102, by reason of defendants' actions which were intended to, and did, interfere with the exercise by plaintiffs, and the members of plaintiff Labor Council, of their rights of free speech and freedom of assembly protected by sec. 101(a) (2) of the Act [29 USC §411(a) (2)].

3. The District Court has jurisdiction under sec. 102 of the Act [29 USC §412] to grant relief to plaintiffs against defendants' violation of sec. 101(a) (2).

4. The District Court reserved consideration and decision on plaintiffs' claim for relief under sec. 101(a) (2):

"Except for our preliminary determination that we have jurisdiction and that the suit is not barred under the exhaustion of remedies doctrine, we come to the question of the validity of President Meany's interpretation of the word 'affiliates,' and all other questions we reserve to be answered on final hearing of this matter." [District Court's Opinion, p. 14]

5. Even though, as decided by this Court, the District Court lacked jurisdiction under sec. 304 of the Act, still, the Court would have jurisdiction under sec. 102 to entertain the action and grant plaintiffs the relief prayed for.

6. Defendants did not challenge the jurisdiction of the District Court under sec. 102, either in the lower Court or in this Court, and plaintiffs' claim for relief under sec. 101(a) (2) and sec. 102 remains to be determined by the District Court.

7. It was well within the discretion of the District Court to issue a preliminary injunction to maintain the status quo pending its final decision on all issues, including plaintiffs' claim for relief under secs. 101(a) (2) and 102, and the granting of such preliminary injunction is subject to review only for abuse of discretion. *Meccano v. John Wanamaker*, 253 U.S. 136, 141 (1920), *Prendergast v. New York Telephone Co.*, 262 U.S. 43 (1923), *Cumberland Telephone and Telegraph Co. v. Louisiana Public Service Commission*, 260 U.S. 212, 219 (1922), *Brotherhood of Locomotive Engineers v. Missouri-Kansas-Texas R. Co.*, 363 U.S. 528, 535 (1960), *Allen W. Hinkel Dry Goods Co. v. Wichison Industrial Gas Co.*, (10th Cir., 1933), 64 Fed. 2d 881, 884.

8. The District Court's finding that the balance of convenience and hardship favors the plaintiffs (Opinion, pp. 13, 15, 16) has not been disturbed by this Court, and the preliminary injunction should therefore be continued pending final decision on plaintiffs' claim under secs. 101(a) (2) and 102 of the Act.

WHEREFORE, plaintiffs-appellees pray that the judgment of this Court be revised so as to remand the case to the District Court for proceedings not inconsistent with this Court's Opinion.

Respectfully submitted,

Philip Hornbein, Jr.

Roy O. Goldin

Attorneys for Plaintiffs-Appellees
1600 Broadway, Suite 1780
Denver, Colorado 80202

Filed on July 3, 1974, the 10th Circuit Court denied the petition for re-hearing one month later. Since the Plaintiffs-Appellees determined not to appeal to the U. S. Supreme Court, the entire determination of judicial judgment is thus complete, even though the Plaintiffs-Appellees consider the Circuit Court judgment to be in error.

Petition denied, August 4, 1974.

APPENDIX B

List of the Unions (1974)

AFL-CIO Affiliated National and International Unions

Actors and Artistes of America, Associated
    165 West 46th Stret   (212)
    New York, N.Y. 10036   245-8295
        This grouping includes the following unions:
        Actor's Equity Association, American Federation of
        Television and Radio Artists, American Guild of
        Musical Artists, American Guild of Variety Artists,
        Screen Actors Guild, Screen Extras Guild)

Air Line Dispatchers Association
    16219 142 Avenue, S.E.   (206)
    Renton, Washington 98055   BA 8-1047

Air Line Pilots Association
    1625 Massachusetts Avenue, N.W.   (202)
    Washington, D.C. 20036   797-4000

Aluminum Workers International Union
    Suite 338, Paul Brown Bldg.
    818 Olive Street   (314)
    St. Louis, Mo. 63101   621-7292

Asbestos Workers, International Association of
    Heat and Frost Insulators and
    505 Machinists Bldg.,
    1300 Connecticut Avenue, N.W.   (202)
    Washington, D.C. 20036   785-2388

Bakery and Confectionery Workers International Union
of America
1828 L Street, N.W., Suite 900   (202)
Washington, D.C. 20036   466-2500

Barbers, Hairdressers and Cosmetologists' International
Union of America, The Journeymen
4755 Kingsway Drive   (317)
Indianapolis, Indiana 46205   257-2255

Boilermakers, Iron Ship Builders, Blacksmiths, Forgers
and Helpers, International Brotherhood of
8th Street at State Avenue   (913)
Kansas City, Kansas 66101   371-2640

Boot and Shoe Workers' Union
1265 Boylston Street   (617)
Boston, Massachusetts 02215   262-5325

Bricklayers, Masons and Plasterers International Union
of America
815 15th Street, N.W.   (202)
Washington, D.C. 20005   783-3788

Brick and Clay Workers of America, The United
83 South 4th Street, Suite 300   (614)
Columbus, Ohio 43215   464-2593

Broadcast Employees and Technicians, National Association of
1601 Connecticut Avenue, N.W.
Suite 420   (202)
Washington, D.C. 20009   265-3601

Carpenters and Joiners of America, United Brotherhood of
101 Constitution Avenue, N.W.   (202)
Washington, D.C. 20001   546-6206

Cement, Lime and Gypsum Workers International Union, United
7830 West Lawrence Avenue   (312)
Chicago, Illinois 60656   457-1177

Chemical Workers Union, International
1655 West Market Street   (216)
Akron, Ohio 44313   867-2444

Cigarmakers' International Union of America
    815 15th Street, N.W., Room 532   (202)
    Washington, D.C. 20005   628-9185

Clothing Workers of America, Amalgamated
    15 Union Square   (212)
    New York, N.Y. 10003   255-7800

Communications Workers of America
    1925 K Street, N.W.   (202)
    Washington, D.C. 20006   337-7711

Coopers International Union of North America
    183 Mall Office Center, 400 Sherburn Lane   (502)
    Louisville, Kentucky 40207   897-3274

Distillery, Rectifying, Wine and Allied Workers,
    International Union of America
    66 Grand Avenue   (201)
    Englewood, New Jersey 07631   569-9212

Dolls, Toys, Playthings, Novelties and Allied Products
    of the United States and Canada, AFL-CIO, International
    Union of
    132 West 43rd Street   (212)
    New York, N.Y. 10036   OX 5-5766

Electrical, Radio and Machine Workers, International
    Union of
    1126 16th Street, N.W.   (202)
    Washington, D.C. 20036   296-1200

Electrical Workers, International Brotherhood of
    1125 15th Street, N.W.   (202)
    Washington, D.C. 20005   833-7110

Elevator Constructors, International Union of
    Suite 1515, 12 South 12th Street   (215)
    Philadelphia, Pa. 19107   922-2226

Engineers, International Union of Operating
    1125 Seventeenth Street, N.W.   (202)
    Washington, D.C. 20036   347-8560

Farm Workers National Union, United
    P.O. Box 47   (805)
    Keene, California 93531   822-5571

Fire Fighters, International Association of
    1750 New York Avenue, N.W.   (202)
    Washington, D.C. 20006   872-8484

Firemen and Oilers, International Brotherhood of
    V.F.W. Bldg., 5th Floor
    200 Maryland Avenue, N.E.   (202)
    Washington, D.C. 20002   547-7540

Flight Engineers' International Association
    905 16th Street, N.W.   (202)
    Washington, D.C. 20006   347-4511

Furniture Workers of America, United
    700 Broadway, 4th Floor   (212)
    New York, N.Y. 10003   477-9150

Garment Workers of America, United
    31 Union Square W., Room 1404   (212)
    New York, N.Y. 10003   WA 4-6860

Garment Workers Union, International Ladies'
    1710 Broadway   (212)
    New York, N.Y. 10019   CO 5-7000

Glass and Ceramic Workers of North America, United
    556 East Town Street   (614)
    Columbus, Ohio 43215   221-4465

Glass Bottle Blowers' Association of the United States
    and Canada
    226 South 16th Street, Room 501   (215)
    Philadelphia, Pa. 19102   KI 5-0540

Glass Cutters League of America, Window
    1078 South High Street   (614)
    Columbus, Ohio 43206   443-2310

Glass Workers Union, American Flint
    1440 South Byrne Road   (419)
    Toledo, Ohio 43614   385-6687

Government Employees, American Federation of
    1325 Massachusetts Avenue, N.W.   (202)
    Washington, D.C. 20005   737-8700

Grain Millers, American Federation of
    4949 Olson Memorial Highway   (612)
    Minneapolis, Minnesota 55422   545-0211

Granite Cutters, International Association of America, The
    18 Federal Avenue   (617)
    Quincy, Massachusetts 02169   472-0209

Graphic Arts International Union
    1900 L Street, N.W.   (202)
    Washington, D.C. 20036   872-7900

Hatters, Cap and Millinery Workers International Union,
    United
    245 5th Avenue   (212)
    New York, N.Y. 10016   683-5200

Horse Shoers of United States and Canada, International
    Union of Journeymen
    8795 S.W. 99th Street   (305)
    Miami, Florida 33156   271-3459

Hotel and Restaurant Employees' and Bartenders' International
    Union
    120 East Fourth Street   (513)
    Cincinnati, Ohio 45202   621-0300

Industrial Workers of America, International Union, Allied
    3520 West Oklahoma Avenue   (414)
    Milwaukee, Wisconsin 53215   645-9500

Insurance Workers International Union, AFL-CIO
    1017 12th Street, N.W.   (202)
    Washington, D.C. 20005   783-1127

Iron Workers, International Association of Bridge
    and Structural
    1750 New York Avenue, N.W., Suite 400   (202)
    Washington, D.C. 20006   872-1566

Jewelry Workers Union, International
    8 West 40th Street, Suite 907-910   (212)
    New York, N.Y. 10018   244-8793

Laborers' International Union of North America
    905 16th Street, N.W.   (202)
    Washington, D.C. 20006   737-8320

Lathers, International Union of Wood, Wire and Metal
    6530 New Hampshire Avenue   (301)
    Takoma Park, Md. 20012   270-1200

Laundry and Dry Cleaning International Union, AFL-CIO
    610 16th Street, Room 421   (415)
    Oakland, California 94612   893-1796

Leather Goods, Plastics and Novelty Workers Union,
    International
    265 West 14th Street, 14th Floor   (212)
    New York, N.Y. 10011   OR 5-9240

Leather Workers International Union of America
    11 Peabody Square   (617)
    Peabody, Massachusetts 01961   531-5605

Letter Carriers, National Association of
    100 Indiana Avenue, N.W.   (202)
    Washington, D.C. 20001   393-4695

Longshoremen's Association AFL-CIO, International
    17 Battery Place, Room 1530   (212)
    New York, N.Y. 10004   425-1200

Machinists and Aerospace Workers, International Association of
    Machinists Bldg., 1300 Connecticut Avenue, N.W.   (202)
    Washington, D.C. 20036   785-2525

Maintenance of Way Employes, Brotherhood of
    12050 Woodward Avenue   (313)
    Detroit, Michigan 48203   868-0489

Marble, Slate and Stone Polishers, Rubbers and Sawyers, Tile
    and Marble Setters Helpers and Terrazzo Helpers,
    International Association of
    Room 628, 821 15th Street, N.W.   (202)
    Washington, D.C. 20005   347-7414

Marine and Shipbuilding Workers of America, Industrial Union of
    1126 16th Street, N.W.   (202)
    Washington, D.C. 20036   223-0902

Marine Engineer's Beneficial Association, National
    17 Battery Place, Room 1930   (212)
    New York, N.Y. 10004   425-7280

Maritime Union of America, National
    36 Seventh Avenue   (212)
    New York, N.Y. 10011   924-3900

Meat Cutters and Butcher Workmen of North America,
    Amalgamated
    2800 North Sheridan Road   (312)
    Chicago, Illinois 60657   248-8700

Mechanics Educational Society of America
    1421 First National Bldg.   (313)
    Detroit, Michigan 48226   965-6990

Metal Polishers, Buffers, Platers and Allied Workers
    5578 Montgomery Road   (513)
    Cincinnati, Ohio 45212   531-2500

Molders and Allied Workers Union, AFL-CIO, International
    1225 East McMillan Street   (513)
    Cincinnati, Ohio 45206   221-1525

Musicians, American Federation of
    1500 Broadway   (212)
    New York, N.Y. 10036   869-1330

Newspaper Guild, The
    1125 15th Street, N.W.   (202)
    Washington, D.C. 20005   296-2990

Office and Professional Employees International Union
    815 16th Street, N.W., Suite 606   (202)
    Washington, D.C. 20006   393-4464

Oil, Chemical and Atomic Workers International Union
    P.O. Box 2812, 1636 Champa Street   (303)
    Denver, Colorado 80201   266-0811

Painters and Allied Trades of the United States and Canada,
    International Brotherhood of
    1750 New York Avenue, N.W.   (202)
    Washington, D.C. 20006   872-1444

Paperworkers International Union, United
    163-03 Horace Harding Expressway   (212)
    Flushing, New York 11365   762-6000

Pattern Makers League of North America
 1000 Connecticut Avenue, N.W., Suite 204   (202)
 Washington, D.C. 20036   296-3790

Plasterers' and Cement Masons' International Association of
 the United States and Canada, Operative
 1125 17th Street, N.W.   (202)
 Washington, D.C. 20036   393-6569

Plumbing and Pipe Fitting Industry of the United States and
 Canada, United Association of Journeymen and Apprentices of the
 901 Massachusetts Avenue, N.W.   (202)
 Washington, D.C. 20001   628-5823

Porters, Brotherhood of Sleeping Car
 1716-18 Seventh Street   (415)
 Oakland, California 94607   TW 3-0894

Postal Workers Union, AFL-CIO, American
 817 14th Street, N.W.   (202)
 Washington, D.C. 20005   683-2304

Pottery and Allied Workers, International Brotherhood of
 P.O. Box 988   (216)
 East Liverpool, Ohio 43920   386-5653

Printers, Die Stampers and Engravers Union of North America,
 International Plate
 3513 Broadway   (212)
 Long Island City, N.Y. 11106   AS 8-5564

Printing Pressman's and Assistants' Union of North America,
 International
 1730 Rhode Island Avenue, N.W.   (202)
 Washington, D.C. 20036   293-2185

Professional and Technical Engineers, International
 Federation of
 1126 16th Street, N.W., Suite 200   (202)
 Washington, D.C. 20036   223-1811

Radio Association, American
 270 Madison Avenue, Room 207   (212)
 New York, N.Y. 10016   689-5754

Railway Carmen of the United States and Canada, Brotherhood of
    4929 Main Street, Carmen's Bldg.   (816)
    Kansas City, Missouri 64112   561-1112

Railway, Airline and Steamship Clerks, Freight Handlers,
    Express and Station Employes, Brotherhood of
    6300 River Road   (312)
    Rosemont, Illinois 60018   692-7711

Railway Supervisors Association, American
    4250 West Montrose Avenue   (312)
    Chicago, Illinois 60641   282-9424

Retail Clerks International Association
    Suffridge Bldg., 1775 K Street, N.W.   (202)
    Washington, D.C. 20006   223-3111

Retail, Wholesale and Department Store Union
    101 West 31st Street   (212)
    New York, N.Y. 10001   947-9303

Roofers, Damp and Waterproof Workers Association, United
    Slate, Tile and Composition
    1125 17th Street, N.W.   (202)
    Washington, D.C. 20036   638-3228

Rubber, Cork, Linoleum and Plastic Workers of America, United
    URWA Building, 87 South High Street   (216)
    Akron, Ohio 44308   376-6181

Seafarers International Union of North America
    675 Fourth Avenue   (212)
    Brooklyn, N.Y. 11232   499-6600

Service Employees International Union, AFL-CIO
    900 17th Street, N.W., Suite 708   (202)
    Washington, D.C. 20006   296-5940

Sheet Metal Workers International Association
    1750 New York Avenue, N.W.   (202)
    Washington, D.C. 20006   296-5880

Shoe Workers of America, United
    120 Boylston Street, Suite 222   (617)
    Boston, Massachusetts 02116   523-6121

Siderographers, International Association of
    1134 Boulevard   (201)
    New Milford, New Jersey 07646   836-9158

Signalmen of America, Brotherhood of Railroad
    601 Golf Road   (312)
    Mount Prospect, Illinois 60056   439-3732

Stage Employees and Moving Picture Machine Operators of the
    United States and Canada, International Alliance of
    Theatrical
    Suite 1900, RKO Building, 1270 Avenue of the Americas   (212)
    New York, N.Y. 10020   245-4369

State, County and Municipal Employees, American Federation of
    Madison Building, 1155 15th Street, N.W.   (202)
    Washington, D.C. 20005   223-4460

Steelworkers of America, United
    Five Gateway Center   (412)
    Pittsburgh, Pennsylvania 15222   562-2400

Stove, Furnace and Allied Appliance Workers of North America
    2929 South Jefferson Avenue   (314)
    St. Louis, Missouri 63118   664-3736

Teachers, American Federation of
    1012 14th Street, N.W.   (202)
    Washington, D.C. 20005   737-6141

Telegraph Workers, United
    10605 Concord Street   (301)
    Kensington, Maryland 20795   942-7877

Textile Workers of America, United
    420 Common Street   (617)
    Lawrence, Massachusetts 01840   686-2901

Textile Workers Union of America
    99 University Place   (212)
    New York, N.Y. 10003   673-1400

Tobacco Workers, International Union of
    1522 K Street, N.W., Suite 616   (202)
    Washington, D.C. 20005   659-1366

Train Dispatchers Association, American
    10 East Huron Street   (312)
    Chicago, Illinois 60611   944-5353

Transit Union, Amalgamated
    5025 Wisconsin Avenue, N.W.   (202)
    Washington, D.C. 20016   537-1645

Transport Workers Union of America
    1980 Broadway   (212)
    New York, N.Y. 10023   873-6000

Transportation Union, United
    15401 Detroit Avenue   (216)
    Cleveland, Ohio 44107   228-3000

Typographical Union, International
    P.O. Box 157   (303)
    Colorado Springs, Colorado 80901   636-2341

Upholsterers' International Union of North America
    25 North Fourth Street   (215)
    Philadelphia, Pennsylvania 19106   WA 3-5700

Utility Workers Union of America
    475 Park Avenue South,   (212)
    New York, N.Y. 10016   685-8730

Woodworkers of America, International
    1622 North Lombard Street   (503)
    Portland, Oregon 97217   285-5281

Yardmasters of America, Railroad
    Schoch Building, Room 201-202
    1411 Peterson Avenue   (312)
    Park Ridge, Illinois 60068   696-2510

State Central Bodies of AFL-CIO

Alabama Labor Council, AFL-CIO
    1018 South 18th Street   (205)
    Birmingham 35205   933-8956

Alaska State Federation of Labor, AFL-CIO
    1035 East 28th Avenue   (907)
    Anchorage 99504   279-6311

Arizona State, American Federation of Labor and
    Congress of Industrial Organizations, AFL-CIO
    2475 East Water Street   (602)
    Tucson 85719   793-9476

Arkansas State AFL-CIO
    1408 Rebsamen Park Road   (501)
    Little Rock 72202   663-4164

California Labor Federation, AFL-CIO
    Suite 310, 995 Market Street   (415)
    San Francisco 94103   986-3585

Colorado Labor Council, AFL-CIO
    360 Acoma, Room 300   (303)
    Denver 80223   733-2401

Connecticut State Labor Council, AFL-CIO
    9 Washington Avenue   (203)
    Hamden 06518   288-3591

Delaware State Labor Council, AFL-CIO
    3031-3033 North Market Street   (302)
    Wilmington 19802   762-3666

Florida AFL-CIO
    P.O. Box 537
    Allapattah Station   (305)
    Miami 33142   634-3961

Georgia State AFL-CIO
    501 Pulliam Street, S.W., Room 549   (404)
    Atlanta 30312   525-2793

Hawaii State Federation of Labor, AFL-CIO
    547 Halekauwila Street, Suite 216   (808)
    Honolulu 96813   536-4945

Idaho State AFL-CIO
    P. O. Box 269   (208)
    Boise 83701   342-2361

Illinois State Federation of Labor and Congress of
    Industrial Organizations
    300 North State Street, 16th Floor   (312)
    Chicago 60610   222-1414

Indiana State AFL-CIO
   1000 North Madison Avenue
   P.O. Box 385   (317)
   Greenwood 46142   881-6773

Iowa Federation of Labor, AFL-CIO
   2000 Walker Street, Suite A   (515)
   Des Moines 50317   262-9571

Kansas State Federation of Labor, AFL-CIO
   3830 South Meridian   (316)
   Wichita 67217   522-1591

Kentucky State AFL-CIO
   706 East Broadway   (502)
   Louisville 40202   584-8189

Louisiana AFL-CIO
   P.O. Box 3477   (504)
   Baton Rouge 70821   343-5747

Maine State Federated Labor Council, AFL-CIO
   499 Broadway   (207)
   Bangor 04401   942-5264

Maryland State and D.C., AFL-CIO
   305 West Monument Street   (301)
   Baltimore 21201   727-7307

Massachusetts State Labor Council, AFL-CIO
   21 Court Street   (617)
   Natick 01760   237-1067

Michigan State AFL-CIO
   1034 North Washington Avenue   (517)
   Lansing 48906   485-4348

Minnesota AFL-CIO
   414 Auditorium Street   (612)
   St. Paul 55102   227-7647

Mississippi AFL-CIO
   P.O. Box 2010   (601)
   Jackson 39205   948-0517

Missouri State Labor Council, AFL-CIO
    208 Madison Street
    P.O. Box 1086   (314)
    Jefferson City 65101   635-6185

Montana State AFL-CIO
    Route 1, South, Box 981   (406)
    Great Falls 59401   453-9444

Nebraska State AFL-CIO
    Labor Temple, 1821 California Street   (402)
    Omaha 68102   345-2500

Nevada State AFL-CIO
    P.O. Box 14396   (702)
    Las Vegas 89114   385-2131

New Hampshire State Labor Council, AFL-CIO
    21 High Street   (603)
    Nashua 03060   889-1128

Nw Jersey State AFL-CIO
    106 West State Street   (609)
    Trenton 08608   989-8730

New Mexico State AFL-CIO
    777 West San Mateo   (505)
    Santa Fe 87501   982-2589

New York State AFL-CIO
    30 East 29th Street   (212)
    New York 10016   689-9320

North Carolina State AFL-CIO
    P.O. Box 10805   (919)
    Raleigh 27605   833-6678

North Dakota AFL-CIO
    1911 North 11th Street   (701)
    Bismarck 58501   223-0784

Ohio AFL-CIO
    271 East State Street   614)
    Columbus 43215   224-8271

Oklahoma State AFL-CIO
    P.O. Box 53567 (405)
    Oklahoma City 73105 528-2409

Oregon AFL-CIO
    316 Portland Labor Center
    201 S.W. Arthur Street (503)
    Portland 97201 224-3768

Pennsylvania AFL-CIO
    101 Pine Street (717)
    Harrisburg 17101 238-9351

Puerto Rico Federation of Labor, AFL-CIO
    P.O. Box 1648 (809)
    San Juan 00903 764-4980

Rhode Island AFL-CIO
    357 Westminster Street (401)
    Providence 02903 861-6600

South Carolina Labor Council, AFL-CIO
    2000 Sumter Street (803)
    Columbia 29201 256-0392

South Dakota State Federation of Labor, AFL-CIO
    101 South Fairfax Avenue (605)
    Sioux Falls 57103 338-3811

Tennessee State Labor Council, AFL-CIO
    226 Capitol Blvd., Room 203 (615)
    Nashville 37219 256-5687

Texas State AFL-CIO
    308 West 11th Street
    P.O. Box 12727 (512)
    Austin 78711 477-6195

Utah State AFL-CIO
    440 South Fourth East (801)
    Salt Lake City 84111 364-7554

Vermont State Labor Council, AFL-CIO
    141 Crescent Street, Box 41 (802)
    Rutland 05701 773-9688

Virginia State AFL-CIO
    3315 West Broad Street   (703)
    Richmond 23230   355-7444

Washington State Labor Council, AFL-CIO
    2700 1st Avenue, Room 206   (206)
    Seattle 98121   MU 2-6002

West Virginia Labor Federation, AFL-CIO
    1624 Kanawha Blvd., East   (304)
    Charleston 25323   344-3557

Wisconsin State AFL-CIO
    6333 West Bluemound Road   (414)
    Milwaukee 53213   771-0700

Wyoming State AFL-CIO
    1904 Thomes Ave.   (307)
    Cheyenne 82001   635-5149

Non-Affiliated American Unions

Aeronautical Examiners, National Association of
    3862 Coleman Avenue   (714)
    Imperial Beach, California 92032   423-4316

Aeronautical Production Controlmen Association
    1572 Rieger Avenue   (415)
    Hayward, California 94544   782-5695

Alaska State Employees Association
    114 South Franklin Street   (907)
    Juneau, Alaska 99801   586-2334

Allied Workers International Union, United
    1085 Broadway Street   (215)
    Gary, Indiana 46402   932-9400

ASCS County Office Employees, National Association of
    Plankinton, South Dakota 57368

Associated Unions of America
    161 West Wisconsin Avenue   (414)
    Milwaukee, Wisconsin 53203   272-2543

Automobile, Aerospace and Agricultural Implement
   Workers of America, International Union, United
    8000 East Jefferson Avenue   (313)
    Detroit, Michigan 48214   926-5201

Baseball Players Association, Major League
    375 Park Avenue   (212)
    New York, N.Y. 10022   752-0940

Basketball Players Association, National
    15 Columbus Circle   (212)
    New York, N.Y. 10023   541-7118

Christian Labor Association of the United States
   of America
    1600 Buchanan Avenue, S.W.   (616)
    Grand Rapids, Michigan 49507   241-1649

Consumers Service Association; National
    806 15th Street, N.W.   (202)
    Washington, D.C. 20005   347-5955

Die Sinkers' Conference, International
    One Erieview Plaza   (216)
    Cleveland, Ohio 44114   522-1050

Directors Guild of America, Inc.
    7950 Sunset Blvd.   (213)
    Hollywood, California 90046   656-1220

Distributive Workers of America, National Council of
    13 Astor Place   (212)
    New York, N.Y. 10003   673-5120

Education Association, National
    1201 16th Street, N.W.   (202)
    Washington, D.C. 20036   833-4314

Electrical, Radio, and Machine Workers of America,
   United
    11 East 51st Street   (212)
    New York, N.Y. 10022   753-1960

Federal Employees, National Federation of
    1737 H Street, N.W.   (202)
    Washington, D.C. 20006   298-6315

Football League Players Association, National
    1300 Connecticut Avenue, N.W.   (202)
    Washington, D.C. 20036   833-3335

Government Employees, National Association of
    285 Dorchester Avenue   (617)
    Boston, Massachusetts 02127   268-5002

Government Inspectors, National Association of
    Route 1, Box 84
    Grantsboro, North Carolina 28529

Guards Union of America, International
    P.O. Box 995   (502)
    La Mesa, California 92041   454-0278

Hockey League Players' Association, National
    365 Bay Street   (416)
    Toronto, Ontario, Canada   366-5375

Independent Unions, Congress of
    303 Ridge Street   (618)
    Alton, Illinois 62002   462-2447

Industrial Workers Union, National
    1201 East Court Avenue   (515)
    Des Moines, Iowa 50316   266-1137

Insurance Agents, International Union of Life
    161 West Wisconsin Avenue   (414)
    Milwaukee, Wisconsin 53203   273-7849

Internal Revenue Employees, National Association of
    1730 K Street, N.W.   (202)
    Washington, D.C. 20005   785-4411

Lace Operatives of America, Amalgamated
    4013 Glendale Street   (215)
    Philadelphia, Pennsylvania 19124   743-9358

Licensed Officers' Organization, Great Lakes
    P.O. Box 387   (616)
    Ludington, Michigan 49431   843-9543

Licensed Practical Nurses, National Federation of
    250 West 57th Street   (212)
    New York, N.Y. 10019   246-6629

Locomotive Engineers, Brotherhood of
    1112 Brotherhood of Locomotive Engineers Building   (216)
    Cleveland, Ohio 44114   241-2630

Longshoremen's and Warehousemen's Union, International
    150 Golden Gate Avenue   (415)
    San Francisco, California 94102   775-0533

Machine Printers and Engravers Association of
the United States
    172 Taunton Avenue   (401)
    East Providence, Rhode Island 02914   438-5849

Mailers Union, International
    Villa Italia Center, Suite 530
    7200 West Alameda Avenue   (303)
    Denver, Colorado 80226   936-6475

Mine Workers of America, United
    900 15th Street, N.W.   (202)
    Washington, D.C. 20005   638-0530

National Labor Relations Board Professional Association
    1717 Pennsylvania Avenue, N.W.   (202)
    Washington, D.C. 20006   382-4841

National Labor Relations Board Union
    1000 Savings Tower, 411 Hamilton Blvd.   (312)
    Peoria, Illinois 61602   353-7604

Nurses' Association, American
    10 Columbus Circle   (212)
    New York, N.Y. 10019   582-7230

Operations Analysis Association, National
    107 Jamacha Blvd.   (714)
    Spring Valley, California 92077   469-9912

Packinghouse and Dairy Workers, National
Brotherhood of
    1201 East Court Avenue   (515)
    Des Moines, Iowa 50316   266-1137

Patent Office Professional Association
    Patent Office   (703)
    Washington, D.C. 20231   557-2577

Planners, Estimators, and Progressmen, National
    Association of
    4005 Rampart Street   (703)
    Virginia Beach, Virginia 23455   464-4515

Plant Guard Workers of America, International
    Union, United
    14214 East Jefferson Avenue   (313)
    Detroit, Michigan 48215   821-1132

Police, Fraternal Order of
    1501 North Miracle Mile Strip   (602)
    Tucson, Arizona, 85705   622-4664

Postal and Federal Employees, National Alliance of
    1644 11th Street, N.W.   (202)
    Washington, D.C. 20001   332-4313

Postal Supervisors, National Association of
    P.O. Box 1924   (202)
    Washington, D.C. 20013   783-7456

Postmasters of the United States, National League of
    955 L'Enfant Plaza, Suite 4400   (202)
    Washington, D.C. 20013   488-8292

Protection Employees, Independent Union of Plant
    122 Pickard Drive   (315)
    Mattydale, New York 13211   454-4518

Quarantine Inspectors National Association,
    Federal Plant
    P.O. Box 9812   (915)
    El Paso, Texas 79988   533-5268

Rural Letter Carriers' Association, National
    1750 Pennsylvania Avenue, N.W.   (202)
    Washington, D.C. 20006   298-9260

Shoe and Allied Craftsmen, Brotherhood of
    838 Main Street   (617)
    Brockton, Massachusetts 02401   587-2606

Teamsters, Chauffeurs, Warehousemen and Helpers
    of America, International Brotherhood of
    25 Louisiana Avenue, N.W.   (202)
    Washington, D.C. 20001   783-0525

Telephone Unions, Alliance of Independent
    P.O. Box 5462   (203)
    Hamden, Connecticut 16518   288-5271

Textile Foremen's Guild, Inc.
    117 Broadway   (201)
    Paterson, New Jersey 07503   684-5092

Tool Craftsmen, International Association of
    3243 37th Avenue   (309)
    Rock Island, Illinois 61201   788-9776

Trademark Society, Inc.
    P.O. Box 2062, EADS Station   (703)
    Arlington, Virginia 22202   557-3275

Umpires Association, Major League
    1 North LaSalle Street   (312)
    Chicago, Illinois 60602   263-3890

University Professors, American Association of
    1 Dupont Circle   (202)
    Washington, D.C. 20036   466-8050

Veterinarians, National Association of Federal
    1522 K Street, N.W.   (202)
    Washington, D.C. 20005   659-2040

Watch Workers Union, American
    617 West Orange Street   (717)
    Lancaster, Pennsylvania 17603   397-1339

Watchmen's Association, Independent
    11 Broadway   (212)
    New York, N.Y. 10004   943-5880

Western Pulp and Paper Workers, Association of
    1430 Southwest Clay   (503)
    Portland, Oregon 97201   228-7486

Writers Guild of America
    Writers Guild of America, East, Inc.
        22 West 48th Street   (212)
        New York, N.Y. 10036   575-5060

    Writers Guild of America, West, Inc.
        8955 Beverly Blvd.   (213)
        Los Angeles, California 90048   274-8601

Index